Joy
IN THE
MOURNING
GROWING THROUGH GRIEF

HAROLD WELTER

ISBN: 978-1-948693-26-4

Library of Congress Control Number: 2023923703

Print information is available on the last page.

Cover design: Waqar Nadeem and Cover Photo: Stephen Vogt

Giving Gal Press Date January 15, 2024 Disclaimer and Limit of Liability

WHAT OTHERS SAY ABOUT
Joy in the Mourning

In an era rife with disbelief and confusion about life, the Cheryl Lyn Welter Charitable Foundation is a tremendous light, and Harold Welter is seeking to restore hope to families—and humanity itself—as he lives out his faith helping others find joy in the mourning.

—Brian Pinson, Pastor, Calvary Baptist Church, Knox, Indiana

Harold Welter, I believe, was sent to me by God at a time I was broken. Our friendship of fifty years took on a new meaning when we lost our daughter, and he helped me find the joy in the mourning, which this book is about. He has used his own heartbreak to help others put their hearts back together, and this book is the blueprint of how it can be done.

—Garry White, Air Force Veteran of the Vietnam era and Father of Rachel

Joy in the Mourning takes me back to the tragedies which have affected not only our own lives but also the lives of so many other parents. It also reinforces the fact that you don't need to go through the loss of a child alone. The book offers help in keeping the faith and certainly gives direction for faith, family, friends, and foreverness.

—Tim Roth, Hall of Fame High School Football Coach and Father of Tyler

Harold's compassion and love shine brightly through his own journey of grief with his beloved daughter, Cheryl. In his powerful words and stories, we all can truly find joy in the mourning!

—*Stacia M. Bolakowski, University Minister, Marian University's Ancilla College*

An amazing book for those who have suffered loss. I'm so thankful Harold decided to share his heart with us!

—*Becky Bailey, Founder, Bela Vita Pregnancy Center for Life*

By sharing his personal story, Harold walks the journey of grief and invites us to walk with him and remember our own. He opens a window through which we can begin to see how deeply grace effects our life experiences, our relationships, our successes, our failures, and our pain. All are places where God speaks to us in the everyday and brings us joy in the mourning.

—*James R. Welter, MDiv, Award-winning Author of* When Winter Comes

I have had the privilege of working as Harold's coach for fifteen years. For the longest time, he never told me about Cheryl and her accident. As the years ticked by, he not only shared her story with me but also set goals to honor her memory. The first was establishing a foundation in her name and then writing this book.

Grief can cripple a person, or it can propel them to live the life a loved one can't and make the most of each day. That is what Harold has done. No matter if you lost a child, a parent, or a dear friend, after reading this book, you'll walk away with an idea of how to find joy in the mourning.

—*Stephanie L. Jones, TEDx Speaker, Coach, Podcaster, and Best-Selling/Award-Winning Author*

DEDICATION

This book is dedicated to
Cheryl's siblings
Susan, Laura, and Nathan,
whom I failed as a father in so many ways, but who
love me anyway

And, to Cheryl,
who continues to teach me how to find
joy in the mourning

JOY IN THE MOURNING GIVES BACK

A portion of the proceeds from every copy of this
book is donated to the
Cheryl Lyn Welter Charitable Foundation to support
teachers who work with underprivileged kids
in rural schools.

CONTENTS

INTRODUCTION

The day when parents lose a child never ends. The pain never goes away. The mourning never stops.

Finding joy in the mourning is about finding yourself during the ultimate grief spawned by the worst thing which can happen to a parent, and it's about establishing or reaffirming your personal beliefs. Ultimately, this book is about finding the courage to not only get on with life but also the courage to improve your life and the lives of others.

This book will ask you to face your own failures but not to wallow in what can't be changed. It will ask you to find the creative juices to evaluate your response to the ultimate tragedy.

In the coming pages, you will be invited to join me on a journey that goes beyond anything perceived by experts in dealing with the loss of a child; that is, evaluating, facing, and dealing with your own personal situation.

There are three aspects of this book that those who choose to embark on the journey will need to experience if they are to find joy in the mourning. First, you'll change your perception of grief, whatever that perception may be. Second, you'll think about your loss in ways you may never have imagined. And third, you'll find ways to go forward through personal growth and commitment to making life better . . . for you and those around you.

Those who have lost children find certain things that are true about the experience. First, it's such an unbelievable experience that your first thought is that you can't get through the ensuing days, weeks, months, and years of your life.

Second, it's virtually impossible to think about the steps you'll need to take if you are going to survive the experience with any form of normal mental health.

Third, the first days of coping, let alone thinking of who needs to be notified, how the funeral will be planned, and how you'll get back to work are so overpowering that you will lose what may be termed common sense and may be prone to making short-term decisions which can have long-term devastating effects.

No matter how long it's been since you experienced this heartrending loss, this book will help you address these issues. The fact is that no matter how long it's been, there will always be issues you will have to deal with which may make you feel that it all happened yesterday. So dealing with those issues, whether it's been several days, a few months, or even years is a challenge which will never go away.

At some point, the realization comes to all who have lost a child that mourning is a permanent state, but this book will help you understand that there are ways of dealing with mourning which can lead to growth if we are open to seeking it in our lives going forward.

One of the first things those who choose to begin this journey with us need to realize is that while having partners on a journey makes it more tolerable and can help us understand things which are part of the journey, in the end, each person is on the journey alone. Each person must evaluate his or her own situation. Each person must make their own decisions as to how to go forward, and each person must figure out where they wish the journey to lead.

Let us embark now on the next steps of that journey of the day that will never end. The journey will not shorten the day. The journey will not end the pain that began on that day of our loss. The journey will not stop the mourning. As you continue this journey, however, this book will give you steps to take to deal with that never-ending day. This book will give you the stories of others who have used the pain to grow in faith, hope and love. This book will also provide you with the necessary tools that can help you find joy in the mourning!

CHAPTER 1

———— ༚༒༙ ————

JOY IN THE MOURNING

Weeping may endure for a night,
But joy *comes* in the morning.

(Psalm 30:5 New King James Version)

October 12, 2000, was the worst day of my life.

It shouldn't have been, as it was homecoming week at Knox, Indiana, High School, and our daughter, Cheryl, was a senior who was highly involved in all the fun activities associated with homecoming in the fall at Indiana high schools.

She caught a two-point conversion pass which helped her Senior Class Powder Puff Football team beat the junior team, which was coached by her brother, Nathan.

Two nights later, she helped coach the senior class Ironman Volleyball team to victory in their tournament. Following that, she and some friends went to another friend's house to put the finishing touches on the senior class float which would be in the homecoming parade downtown the next day.

After they finished, she jumped in her car and headed home.

She never made it. Not thinking, she blew through a stop sign, not wearing a seatbelt, and slammed into a semi-truck. She was killed instantly.

Every parent who loses a child wonders where life will lead them without that child. What I have learned is that our mourning never ends, but that there are ways of finding joy in that mourning.

Cheryl's sister, Laura, was a student at St. Mary's College, located just over fifty miles from our home. She lived on campus and rarely came home except on weekends, but, for some reason, she came home that afternoon and went to the volleyball tournament with us.

After the game was over, Laura; her mom, Becky; and I all waved goodbye to Cheryl and left the gym. Cheryl's brother, Nathan, had left earlier after his junior team got beat and went home.

Laura and Becky also went home, but I went to the local radio station to finish some interview editing which I would be using that weekend. Sportscasting had been my original career, but, after about eight years, I took a position as a press secretary for a United States congressman in Washington, DC, for a couple of years before returning home and starting my own financial advisory firm.

I was fortunate that WKVI Radio invited me to return as a sportscaster covering local high school sports. What had been a career became my hobby, so by the time Cheryl and Nathan were in high school, I had been covering local sports for thirty-five years on the radio, so going back to the station to do some preparation for a Saturday sports show which I hosted was not an unusual occurrence.

I quickly finished the editing and headed home, a mile-and-a-half drive, which took me past the local hospital. As I drove by, I noticed a medical helicopter had landed at the hospital and still had its props turning. I didn't take special note of it because the local hospital often transferred patients via helicopter to other hospitals which had more acute care available.

When I arrived at home and went inside, no one was there. I thought that was odd since Becky, Laura, and Nathan had all headed there from the gymnasium. As I drove back past the hospital, I noticed that Nathan's van was ahead of me and pulled into the parking lot at the radio station. Figuring he must be looking for me, thinking I was still at the station, I pulled in behind him and, as soon as I stopped, Nathan jumped out of the van and rushed toward me saying, "Cheryl's dead!"

I asked what happened, he said it was a car accident then, crying, he said, "I just lost my best friend!"

The shock I felt was indescribable. Nathan, Becky, and Laura had just left the hospital so, even though nothing could be done, we returned to Cheryl's bedside. At some point, we called our associate pastor at our church, St. Thomas Aquinas Catholic Church, Msgr. Richard Zollinger. He was filling in for our newly appointed pastor, who was away on vacation. Father Z, as he was called, came immediately to talk and pray with us.

As we were saying our last goodbyes, the phone rang. It was the Red Cross. The woman on the other end told me something I didn't know about our daughter—that when she had gone to get her driver's license the year before, she had volunteered to be an organ donor should something ever happen to her. That was something we had never talked about as a family, or, frankly, ever given any thought to, but, for some reason, it was important to Cheryl.

While I didn't know about her decision, it didn't surprise me because Cheryl was a "people person." She loved helping people, especially those who she felt didn't have it as good as she did.

When Cheryl was growing up, we had a constant stream of kids coming through our house, grazing at our table, and bouncing down our stairs having fun. Some stayed as long as three months because they had nowhere else to go, and they knew that Cheryl cared!

I wear her organ donor pin every day of my life as a reminder of how much she cared for people in need. It reminds me that because she cared about helping other people, there is a person walking around literally seeing the world through Cheryl's eyes.

Cheryl had been accepted into Purdue University's School of Child and Family Counseling. She was planning to make a career out of helping people!

The next few hours were a blur. We had to decide whom to call, what to say, and how to make it known to our family and Cheryl's friends.

Cheryl's grandmother, Becky's mom, lived just three blocks from the hospital, so we made the decision to go there to share the sad news with her first. We also decided to start making phone calls from her house. With the haze that hovered over us, I can't remember all the contacts which were made or who, besides me, made some of the calls, but we contacted the high school principal, Jim Condon, whose daughter, Kristin, was one of Cheryl's very best friends. It just so happened that some other friends were at their house as well.

My business partner, Charlie Hasnerl, came to the house along with his dad, who was a pastor at another local church.

We also had to tell Cheryl's oldest sister, Susan, who was living in Washington, DC. She was working as a congressional assistant, a position she obtained immediately after graduating from college the previous spring. We decided that we didn't want to have to tell her over the phone, so I called my brother Jim, who had experience in counseling since he received a degree in theology after going back to college in his mid-fifties, and asked if he would fly out to Washington to tell Susan in person and bring her back to Indiana. And that's a story in itself, which Jim tells like this:

It was 9:00 p.m. The phone rang. In a controlled voice and measured tone usually reserved for his radio broadcasts, my brother reported the sad news: "Cheryl was killed tonight!"

My niece Cheryl was the youngest of three girls in my brother's family.

"She ran a stop sign and was hit by a semi," he continued. "Could you go to Washington, tell [her sister] Susan, and bring her home? It's not something we want her to hear about over the phone."

I was irritated that the much-touted "bereavement flight" was no less expensive than a regular flight, but I was at Reagan International Airport in DC by 10:30 the next morning. I called Susan for directions to the Rayburn House Office Building, where she worked as a congressional assistant. I ended the conversation quickly, so she didn't have a chance to ask why I was in town.

The Rayburn Building was a short walk from the subway. It was a large building taking up a full block. I walked around that block three times knowing that once I went inside, Susan's life would never be the same. "I need words. Lord, give me the words!" I prayed.

The receptionist called Susan to the lobby, and I asked if there was some place we could talk in private. Susan was cheery and happy to see someone from home, not dreaming of the bad news that I came to share. She sat on a couch, and I sat on a living room type chair next to it.

"So, what's up?" she asked with a smile.

"There's been an accident."

The smile faded from her face. "Was it MeMaw?"

"No, it wasn't Me Maw.

She stood. "Was it Cheryl?"

A curt yes was the only word I could get out.

"Was she hurt?"

Silence   .

A wide-eyed disbelieving look: "She's not she's not."

I mumbled, "I'm sorry."

That was followed by a loud blood-curdling scream: "*Nooo*!" And then sobbing, as the reality set in:"But she was going to come out for a visit."

The receptionist took us to Susan's apartment for clothes, then to the airport. It was about noon, but there were no flights with available seats until 5:00 p.m. But I had been working at St. Monica Parish in Indianapolis as a pastoral associate for several years and had learned about the power of the collar! I also had learned that my title of pastoral associate was usually misread as associate pastor!

"Look," I said as I presented my business card to the ticket agent. "There's been a death in the family, and I need to get this young lady on the next flight to Indianapolis.

"Yes, Father. Is business class okay?"

Susan didn't talk much during the flight or during the two-hour drive up to Knox. As we approached town, she quietly said: 'Take me to the football game; that's where my family will be!"

———— ★ ★ ★ ————

We have found that the grief never ends, but we have also discovered that there can be joy in the most devastating circumstances, and, in this book, we're going to share how you, too, can find that joy.

REFLECTIONS: Chapter 1

• What do you remember most about your child's character?

_____

_____

_____

_____

• What would you most want to share about your child with those who offer their condolences?

_____

_____

_____

_____

• Outside of your immediate family, who was one person who helped you during those first two to three days after your child died?

_____

_____

_____

_____

CHAPTER 2

ฺงฺ

WHAT IS GRIEF?

If we are to find joy in the mourning, we must first understand the meaning of mourning and how it is related to grief.

I had experienced grief in my life before we lost our daughter, Cheryl, but nothing prepared me for the unique kind of grief which comes with the loss of a child, or, at least, I wasn't able to apply anything I might have learned about grief in the throes of grappling with this special kind of grief. I was fortunate to have read a paper written by my older brother, James R. Welter, for a college class he was taking on the challenge of defining grief. This, in part, is what he wrote:

"The terms bereavement, grief, and mourning are often used synonymously in dealing with grief. To clarify the topic, it is important to note the distinction among them.

Bereavement represents the experiential state one endures after realizing a loss. While bereavement represents the state of loss, grief represents the reactions on experiences while in that state. Grief is the thoughts and feelings that are experienced within oneself. It is the internal meaning given to the experience of bereavement. One can experience bereavement without grief. That is to say, one can experience a loss without a related emotion. Conversely, one would not experience the emotion of grief without first being bereaved, that is, without suffering a loss.

Mourning is taking the internal experience of grief and expressing it outside of oneself. It represents the culturally defined acts that are usually performed after a death.[1"]

Sigmund Freud coined the term "object loss" to describe losing something or someone to whom one is attached. Grief breaks the bond between the subject (the survivor) and the object (that which is lost). In reality, then, we grieve for ourselves, the survivor since the object (the deceased) is not capable of grief. We have been deprived of something to which we are attached, and we grieve the loss.[2]

One of the efforts I have made to help others who have experienced the death of a child as we have is to urge them to find joy in their mourning by remembering the good things which they enjoyed with their lost child. Even those who have lost children who were taken at a very young age can remember the child's beautiful smile or bright eyes. Others, such as us, who lost their children after having them to interact with for a good number of years have many more ways of remembering pleasant experiences with their child.

One thing which we learned through the loss of a child is that there are various kinds of grief.

Doug Manning, a grief counselor, pastor, and author, reports that patients often seek confirmation that one type of grief hurts more than another. The death of a child, they will maintain, "hurts more" than the death of an aged parent or the pain of someone who's child was taken instantaneously, as was our Cheryl, hurts more than when the parents can see it coming.[3] Our friend, Al Breyfogle, and his wife, Sharon, watched their son, Brad, go through nine years of pain, surgeries, and uncertainty and so had years to prepare for what they knew was inevitable.

Our friends Tim and Melinda Roth, whose son was killed in an auto accident just seven months after we lost Cheryl, spent thirty-four hours at the hospital bedside of their son, Tyler, before he passed away following a car crash, so they had at least some time (albeit not much) to prepare for his upcoming passing. But did their experience of being able to prepare for the inevitable make their pain any less than ours? Manning, in his writings, rightly states that one type of loss does not "hurt more" than another."[4]

Erich Lindemann coined the term "anticipatory grief." It refers to the absence of overt manifestations of grief at the actual time of death in survivors who have already experienced the normal phases of grief.[5]

This may happen when the survivors see the end coming, and several studies indicate that those who have a period of pre-death bereavement may manage their grief better than those who have no advanced warning of the loss.[6] Anticipatory grief provides the opportunity to deal with any unfinished business, which will help later in the healing process. Unfortunately, the definition of handling grief "better" is never really defined. It brings back Manning's conclusion that "there is no way to compare the grief that results from each type of loss."[7]

When viewing grief and mourning through the eyes of researchers, one can come to his or her own conclusions about what they are going through as someone who has lost a loved one.

The conclusions that come to me are several: First, the loss of a child is different than any other kind of loss and, second, each person may view the loss differently and, therefore, may grieve differently. My wife, Becky, and I have found this to be true.

The way I have dealt with the loss of Cheryl is markedly different than how Becky has approached it. This has been true from the first minute we learned of her death and continues to the present.

We were warned that there was an extremely high divorce rate among couples who have lost a child. Years before, I had heard from a friend who had lost a son that the divorce rate was more than 70 percent or higher. Indeed, Harriet Schiff in 1977 wrote in *The Bereaved Parent* that as high as 90 percent of all bereaved couples are in serious marital difficulty within months after the death of their child.[8] She did not cite her source for that, but at the time we lost Cheryl, no one ever questioned that and so it was presented as fact in many circles. But research since then indicated that that was not necessarily true.[9]

In 2006, The Compassionate Friends, a counseling group, commissioned a survey, and one of the questions dealt with divorce. It was found that only 16 percent of the parents divorce after the death of a child and only 4 percent said it was because of the death, that there were problems in the marriage long before the child died.[10]

I tended to believe the higher number after a good friend of mine lost his only son and told me that he knew the marriage was over within days after the accident. We often told people that we could believe the higher figure because we could see how the different ways we dealt with the grief led to disagreements misunderstandings which could multiply and fester if the couple didn't make a concerted effort to not let the grieving process interfere with the stability of the marriage.

In retrospect, as we've met more people who have lost children, and I've often served as a shoulder to lean on with parents who have more recently lost children, I have witnessed far more people who have grown closer after the loss than those who have split farther apart.

———— ★ ★ ★ ————

Understanding grief and how it applies to you and your loss is one important key to finding joy in the mourning!

REFLECTIONS: Chapter 2

• What is the last positive memory you have of your loved one before they died?

_____

_____

_____

_____

• What advice would you give others who experience a loss such as yours which could make the transition more bearable?

_____

_____

_____

_____

• Name two people who have lost a child who you will encourage.

_____

_____

_____

_____

⸱☙⸱

CHAPTER 3

WALKING THROUGH GRIEF

Going through the grieving process is different for everyone and while many, perhaps most, people have encountered the loss of a loved one, those who have lost a child are not nearly so numerous. So the counsel one could use at this time is perhaps not as available as for other losses, and the first few days after we lost Cheryl were nothing but a blur.

As difficult as it is, thinking clearly about what needs to be done in the early hours, days, and weeks is important if grievers are to find joy in the mourning.

In retrospect, it was probably a good thing that losing Cheryl came at a busy time for her, our family, and a community that was collectively grieving the loss.

It was homecoming week and the highlight of high school homecoming in Indiana is the football game. Other events, such as the judging of class floats and the naming of the homecoming royalty, were also eagerly anticipated. In addition, at that time, the Knox High School Marching Band was a state powerhouse and in the middle of state competition. So what happened immediately after Cheryl's death on Thursday night was a whirlwind of activities, decisions to be made, and the execution of what the student participants had practiced for all year.

The first decision which had to be made was, considering the tragedy which had affected Cheryl's friends and fellow students, would the homecoming events planned for that Friday night, including the football game, even go on? School officials approached Cheryl's mom and me and asked whether we would like the game and other activities to be cancelled. While we were appreciative of being asked, we didn't hesitate to say the activities needed to go on. After all, many of Cheryl's friends were involved, including members of the football team, the homecoming court, and members of the marching band, who were led by her brother, Nathan, as the featured soloist in the show that would be taken to regional competition the following day.

Nathan, to his credit, saved the weekend for his fellow students, team members, and the entire community with a step of leadership that no one asked him to take but that he decided for himself. He went to school the morning after the accident! That step alone showed a level of courage that exhibited his belief that life goes on and that he would show other young people that this was the course to follow any time life throws you a challenge!

His high school principal told us later that day at the homecoming pep rally that as soon as Nathan walked in the door that morning, you could see an immediate change in the atmosphere at the school. He said you could almost feel a shared sigh of relief from the entire student body!

So the afternoon homecoming parade and pep rally were held, and Becky and I attended, along with Cheryl's sister Laura. Cheryl's sister Susan and my brother Jim were still traveling back to Indiana from Washington, DC.

For my part, I was to have a dual role on homecoming night. The school had just built a new football stadium and the homecoming game was to be the first game ever played at the brand-new facility. And, because construction of the new field was behind schedule, the team had not had a home game all season, so in addition to celebrating homecoming, it was also going to be the night that all the fall sport athletes who were seniors would be recognized on Senior Night. Since Cheryl was a senior manager for the volleyball team, she was to be recognized, along with her parents, in pregame ceremonies. Traditionally, the senior athletes meet their parents at midfield and give their mom a rose. The crowd in attendance applauds in recognition, and the festivities are placed on pause so that pictures can be taken of each family. Nathan decided that he would represent his sister and present the rose to his mom. Laura accompanied Becky and me onto the field, and, for a reason I don't know, I carried Cheryl's high school letter jacket onto the field with us.

My other responsibility was that I was scheduled to broadcast the game on the local radio station. I had started a career in radio broadcasting thirty-five years before, and even though I had left radio as a profession, I still broadcast high school sports as my hobby. The question was, would I have enough in me to be able to describe the game for the listeners as if I were feeling no grief? Becky and I made the decision that I would broadcast because the game had so much significance for Cheryl's brother, her legion of friends, and the entire community. So, after the pregame Senior Night activities ended, I slipped on Cheryl's letter jacket and went to the broadcast booth to broadcast the first-ever game on the new field, a field which I had helped assure the construction of as a member of the school board.

To my amazement (and probably to the amazement of our listeners), the broadcast of the game went as normal. I consciously avoided referring to Cheryl's death during the coverage of the game, that is, until our daughter Susan came into the broadcast booth, fresh from her trip from Washington with her uncle Jim. The tears flowed quickly, but, fortunately, her appearance came during our halftime show, which was dominated by my broadcast partners—Charlie Hasnerl, my partner in our financial advising firm, Financial Partners, and long-time friend Dean Dorman—who were used to filling the halftime show with statistics and analysis of the first half. So they were able to keep it normal for the listeners.

Toward the end of the game, which Knox lost, I made a quick reference to the tragedy, thanked the community for their support, and commented that Cheryl had the best seat in the house for her final homecoming game of her high school career.

———— ★ ★ ★ ————

Dealing with grief, both in the short and long term, is a combination of practical steps which need to be taken and emotional steps which are an ongoing part of the journey.

I had made it through the toughest twenty-four hours of my life, partially, I realized later, doing what may be described as "normal" things. Broadcasting football games on Friday nights was what I had done for thirty-five years, so that normality was a positive, which probably helped me get through the coming days and weeks. But getting through those first twenty-four hours could not change what would happen in the next 120 hours as we struggled to find joy in the mourning!

REFLECTIONS: Chapter 3

• What do you remember most about the first twenty-four hours after your loss?

_____

_____

_____

• Name one positive thing that affected you in the first twenty-four hours.

_____

_____

_____

• Name three people who helped you the most in the early hours and days after your loss.

_____

_____

_____

• Write down what you will do to thank those people in the next seven days.

_____

_____

_____

CHAPTER 4

ɔ ɷ ʕ

STAGES OF GRIEF

An American Dictionary of English Language defines grief as "keen mental suffering or distress over affliction or loss."[11] It does not say what that loss entails. We're talking about the death of a child in this context, but loss could be any dramatic change in our life. Loss can be associated with the loss of a job, loss of a spouse via a divorce, physical impairment, or other dramatic changes. We grieve over loss, whatever that loss may be. And, regardless of the nature of the loss, experts have concluded that there are stages of grief.

In her book *On Death and Dying*, author Elisabeth Kübler-Ross maintained that there are five stages of grief. In its simplest form, she defined the stages as denial, anger, bargaining, depression, and acceptance.[12] Others, such as American psychiatrist Erich Lindemann, tend to agree with this view of the stages of grief.[13]

Having gone through the loss of a child, I tend to agree with those assumptions. I also believe that there can be a sixth stage, but that sixth stage must be chosen by the person who is grieving. That sixth stage is *growth*!

According to experts, no matter the nature of the loss which we are grieving, everyone goes through these five stages, whether we recognize them or not.[14] The most important part of getting through these stages is recognizing that they don't necessarily come in the same order for everyone. In my own case, it took me a long time to realize that this was true.

Many months after we lost Cheryl and after I had read my brother Jim's college paper numerous times, I realized that I had experienced four of the five steps. I knew I had gone through denial for a brief period, and I was still experiencing depression, I had wrestled with bargaining, and I knew I would be working on the acceptance phase for a long time. However, I contended that I had not experienced anger.

I had sent a message to the semitruck driver involved in the accident specifically saying that we did not hold him responsible (although I learned some twenty years later that he was still grieving Cheryl's death). I had specifically told people that I was not angry at God as I worked to understand His plan for my life and how this tragedy may fit into that plan. I wasn't angry at her friends who went with her to put the finishing touches on the homecoming float. No, I told myself, I had not experienced the anger phase at all! It took me a long time to realize that wasn't true.

I've always been involved in high school sports. But I wasn't a very good athlete in high school; indeed, to call me a high school "athlete" would be a real stretch of the definition! But I was always an interested observer, and covering local high school sports on the radio was one of my true joys. So, when I was elected to the Knox School Board, I was especially interested in helping the Athletic Department build a successful sports program in the Knox schools.

In that context, the high school athletic director (AD) is responsible for the sports programs, and I always listened carefully to what the AD was doing to make the sports teams more competitive. Our athletic director at the time was a guy named Phil Owens. Phil had been a star record-setting football player in his days as a Knox high school athlete, and he came back to serve as AD because he loved Knox sports. In addition, he was very efficient at his job and often received kudos for the job he was doing, not only from the coaches who collaborated with him but also from the officials and athletic directors of opposing schools.

At some point, many months after we had lost Cheryl, AD Owens described his approach to one of the things he was seeking to change which would, in his estimation, make the program better over time. I disagreed with the plan he outlined, and for nearly six months, I challenged his approach and pleaded with my fellow Board members to ask him to change what he was doing.

In the end, what he was proposing wasn't that big of a move that the Board would even have wanted to change anything about it. Indeed, all these years later, I can't honestly even remember what the issue was that I had constantly badgered him about. About six months into this uncalled-for tirade, I suddenly realized that I was uncharacteristically upset about something that really didn't matter in the grand scheme of things. It was then that I realized I was taking out my anger on someone who had no idea of what was on my plate!

It was so unimportant that when I apologized to Mr. Owens about my behavior, he didn't even seem to know what I was talking about. This was a self-learned lesson about the stages of grief, and, make no mistake about it, when you lose a child, you *will* go through the stages of grief, whether you recognize them at the time or not!

From this early experience in understanding grief, I learned a lesson, and it was one of the early examples of my experiencing the sixth stage of grief, growth!

— ★ ★ ★ —

Experiencing growth and understanding how it might apply to your situation is a major step in finding joy in the mourning!

REFLECTIONS: Chapter 4

• What stages of grief were you most aware of at the time you lost your child?

_____

_____

_____

_____

• What have you done to deal with those stages of grief?

_____

_____

_____

_____

• Name one other person, not related to your child, who was adversely affected by your child's death.

_____

_____

_____

_____

CHAPTER 5

———— ୬୧୨ ————

LIFE GOES ON

If you are to experience the growth stage of grief, it's important to examine your feelings, especially in the early hours, days, weeks, and months following your loss. If it has been longer than a few months, you still need to examine your feelings so that you can start the growth stage from where you currently are.

While the first twenty-four hours after Cheryl's death went by in a blur, the seed was planted for future growth. The reason that I can say that is those twenty-four hours were filled with people helping us deal with the tragedy and with the more positive things which were happening during homecoming. The message we received from all those things was that, even with the most tragic thing which parents could ever go through, life goes on, and it can go on with positives. It took a long time to understand what "life goes on" really means to those experiencing such a tragedy. Over time, we learned that if we were to experience growth from this experience, we had to find positives in the experience.

———— ★ ★ ★ ————

Following the homecoming activities of the previous day, on Saturday, there were more challenges for Cheryl's friends, the Knox High School community, and especially for her brother, Nathan. The Knox High School Marching Band was scheduled to perform in regional competition at Elkhart Central High School, more than sixty miles away.

Marching band competition in Indiana is a big deal, with three levels of competition at that time, beginning with district competition, where teams with the best scores moved on to regional competition. That's where state finalist bands are selected at several sites around the state.

The Redskin Brigade, as the marching band was called, had done well in preliminary competition in the weeks leading up to state competition, as they had scored extremely well in district competition the week before. That advanced them to the regional competition. To advance to the state competition, however, the band would be facing its toughest competition of the year.

Heading into the regional round, no one could predict how the teenagers would react to Cheryl's death when they got on the field, especially with her brother having a key role as the featured trumpet soloist. Would they be able to focus enough to give a state-qualifying performance, or would they be so distracted by the events of the past thirty-six hours that a top-level performance was out of reach? Even after the band arrived at the field and prepared their uniforms, instruments, and field decorations before going through their pre-performance warmup, no one could predict what would happen during the ten-minute performance on the field. Fans, directors, adult field-crew members, and families couldn't predict what would happen in a performance which required more than a hundred band members to be on key with dozens of different instruments and stay in step with a complicated routine, which took each member all over the field, all the while showing that they were having fun!

As the band took the field, those of us working as the field crew at field level held our breath, hoping (and yes, *praying*) for the best performance possible. While we had witnessed the band performing all year, this performance, we knew, was different. There was additional pressure on the kids performing because of the loss of Cheryl. There certainly was additional pressure on her brother, Nathan, as he had become the absolute leader on the field. All eyes were on him as he unleashed his trumpet solo as never before, showing the band that he was there for them just as they had shown in so many ways that they were there for him.

I was told by some of the band members later that they felt good going out onto the field, and when Nathan ended his solo, they knew it was going to be the performance of the year!

Indeed, the performance was virtually flawless, and when the scores from other regional competitions around the state came in, the Redskin Brigade had the best score in the entire state. As the band left the field, I ran to give Cheryl's friend Hannah Looney, one of the student directors responsible for keeping the music together, a hug and congratulate her on her leadership. She triumphantly yelled, "We *did* it!" She later told a newspaper reporter that she felt Cheryl was on her shoulder for the entire performance.

When the final scores were given and the state qualifying bands were named, Knox High School sat at the top of an outstanding field. The pride the band members, their families, and the Knox community felt was indescribable! The feeling on the trip back was so positive, anyone who didn't know about the tragedy the community had suffered a day and a half before could have never guessed that anything but the performance was on the mind of those super-successful teenagers!

What happened when the band took the field in front of thousands of fans was this: they performed flawlessly, giving their best performance of the year, perhaps the best performance in the history of the Knox High School Marching Band!

Once again, in the shadow of the worst tragedy we could imagine, we learned that life does go on, and, unknown to us, we would continue to get those signals in the years that followed.

——— ★ ★ ★ ———

Looking for and experiencing those moments which strongly indicate that life does go on can give you the strength to grow and find joy in the mourning.

REFLECTIONS: Chapter 5

• Looking back on the immediate few days after your loss, what one thing occurred that may have helped you to see that life goes on?

_____

_____

_____

_____

• What is one way you can help others deal with the feelings of those first days, weeks, and months after a loss such as yours?

_____

_____

_____

_____

• Name one thing you read (a book, scripture, or other writings) in the early days following your loss that helped you find comfort.

_____

_____

_____

_____

CHAPTER 6

FROM GRIEF TO FAITH

The five steps of grief, we came to learn, came and went with no consistency. Different people go through the steps in different ways and at different times. Sometimes, those who are going through the steps don't realize until later that what they were feeling had to do with those steps. The challenge becomes recognizing those steps and learning to deal with them as they occur. If you are to experience the sixth step, growth, it's important to remember as much as you can about the things which happened in the immediate aftermath of losing your child so that you can gauge how far you've come on the journey.

We who profess to be Christians, that is, followers of Christ, purport to believe in certain things promised in scripture. Following those beliefs can be easy until the circumstances of life challenge them.

For instance, most of us have said that we believe that God has a plan for our lives, even citing chapter and verse in scripture that spells that out. We may even voice the belief that the plan means that everything happens for a reason, and that makes our lives have purpose. But that contention is challenged beyond comprehension when we lose a child.

Losing a child doesn't make sense in our perception of life. It seems like everything happens (or should have happened) in a logical sequence. That logical sequence is that grandparents should die before parents, and parents should die before their children do.

As the youngest of seven children in my family, I never thought a lot about the sequence of life. I think I just assumed my six siblings would all pass away before me, starting with the oldest and going down to the youngest! When the middle child, our sister Fran, died first at the age of fifty-two, five years before Cheryl died, it was like we were shocked. So when we are hit with dramatic events, the tendency is to look for consistency in our lives.

One of the consistencies in my life for the previous eight years was that I taught confirmation class to high schoolers at our church. Confirmation is one of the seven sacraments recognized by the Catholic Church as essential steps a Christian can take to grow in their faith. It is the person confirming that he or she believes in certain truths and is willing to follow the teachings of Jesus for eternity. Confirming that they will follow the teachings of Jesus, I explain to my students, is the most crucial decision they will ever make. The reason being that it won't always be easy to follow up on that commitment, but, if they do, it can lead them to benefitting from all of the promises Jesus has made to His followers.

The confirmation classes at our parish are held on Sunday mornings. On the Sunday morning following Cheryl's death, I made the decision that class would be held as usual. Perhaps I made the decision to provide some consistency in my life at a time when it all had been taken away. Perhaps I made the decision because I saw it as an opportunity to talk with the young people who were about to make the most important decision of their lives what the Christian faith is all about. Perhaps it was a combination of those things which led me to hold class even though, a few hours later, Cheryl's wake would be held at a local funeral home.

I wish I had recorded the confirmation class discussion that day because I don't clearly remember a lot about it, but I do know that we talked about how death and life happen in God's timeline and His time frame and that we have to learn about our lives and our faith in tough times as well as in good times. Tears were shed and hugs were shared as each of us began to look inside ourselves as to what it all meant. I hoped that I had shared something with these teenagers that would help them in their lives, both then and in the future. Though I didn't realize it at the time, this was another step in a journey of understanding God's plan for my life.

Within a few hours after the confirmation class ended, the wake for Cheryl was scheduled to begin. Becky and I went to the funeral home an hour before visitors were scheduled to begin arriving. When we walked in the front door, a woman we didn't recognize was waiting in the lobby area with a message that would affect my approach to working through the grieving process for the rest of my life.

Su Clark introduced herself and said, "You don't know me, but I just had to be here."

She had driven from her home, nearly seventy miles away, and she explained that our paths had crossed even though we didn't know it. Her daughter, Chelsea, was an outstanding tennis player at Jimtown High School, which was in the same athletic conference as Knox High School, where Cheryl was on the team. In fact, both were scheduled to be playing in the number-one singles spot for their respective teams their senior year. Su explained that her daughter had died in an auto accident the previous spring, and she knew that Chelsea and Cheryl would have been playing for the conference championship in what would have been their senior season.

The visit was so unexpected and so unselfish of her that we were overwhelmed. Her gesture stuck with me and became the basis on how I would try to help grieving parents going forward. Little did we know that within a matter of a few months, we would pattern ourselves after Su, as we would be comforting dear friends of ours who lost their son who was in the same year of high school as Chelsea and Cheryl!

After Su left and Cheryl's siblings arrived, it was a struggle to get past the grief as we saw Cheryl lying in the coffin, wearing her brother's torn football jersey, where people would come to pay their respects. And had I been more attentive, I would have been much more cognizant of the needs of her siblings in the days, weeks, and months that followed.

As we began greeting visitors who came to pay their respects, we were overwhelmed by the sheer numbers. As it turned out, the line of visitors continued for nine hours straight, without a letup. The funeral director later told us that it was the biggest turnout their facility had ever seen for a funeral in their fifty-four years of existence! The response was proof of what a people person Cheryl was and how she endeared herself to others.

Later, we found joy in our mourning as we realized that Cheryl took it upon herself to really get to know people. Countless young people came to us with the same sentiment: dozens and dozens of her peers told us that "Cheryl was my best friend." It was a real blessing for us to know that Cheryl treated people so well, they all thought that she was their best friend!

Some hours into the wake, we asked my brother Jim to hold a short commemorative service. His theology degree served him well, as he conducted the service in a manner which caused numerous people to tell us afterward that they had never had quite an experience such as that. Frankly, we thought the service might signal the end to the wake, but, instead, people continued to wait in line for another three hours!

What was ironic was that while Cheryl's wake was being conducted, a wake was being held at another funeral home across town for my former high school business teacher. Norm McCurdy was the best teacher I ever had, and he died on the same day as Cheryl when he was struck by a train. Later, we found that there were many things which happened on October 12, locally, nationally, and internationally, which would be brought to our attention and touch our lives for years to come.

The next day, the funeral was held in the church where Cheryl had been baptized as an infant. It was also where she had received the sacrament of confirmation, pledging to follow Jesus. The church was packed with hundreds of her friends as well as our family friends.

Then, on a beautiful October afternoon, she was laid to rest in the local cemetery in a plot near where her grandfather, Becky's dad, had been buried ten years before. Hundreds of people then came back to the church for a luncheon, where we received more kind words and gestures from friends and family.

The day after the funeral gave us the first sign that God was with us in our sorrow and confirmed what I had always believed—that there's no such thing as "coincidence!" Indeed, I learned to believe that God doesn't do coincidence. Everything happens for a reason and as part of God's plan.

When I went out to the mailbox across the street from our house to get the mail, I was astonished to find hundreds of cards wishing us well, expressing sympathy for our loss. I took the cards into the house and, as I laid them on the table, I realized that we didn't have a letter opener!

I no sooner realized that than the phone rang. My business partner, Charlie, told me I had received a gift in the mail at the office from one of the companies with which we did business at our financial advisory firm, and he said he would bring it right down to our house. When he arrived with the gift, I was absolutely shocked as I recognized the significance of the gift. In recognition of the amount of business we had submitted to the company, they gave me an engraved, gold-plated letter opener!

As it turned out, this was one of several things which happened that we took as signs from Cheryl that she was still with us. As we used the gift to open the seemingly endless number of cards we received that day and for several days after, we were thankful to receive this practical gift which conveyed such a message to us!

While the day after the funeral was made lighter by that unexpected gift and was spent reading and appreciating the many, many cards and letters of support, nothing could have prepared us for what happened the following day.

On the Wednesday following the funeral, we were pleasantly surprised to get a visit from a friend from long ago that we didn't expect. Sister Roberta Christensen had been a teacher at St. Anne's Catholic School, where Cheryl had begun her elementary school education. She had since gone to pursue her vocation in Europe and had just recently returned and, hearing about Cheryl's death, came to give us support.

We had hardly begun our conversation reminiscing about Cheryl's early education and the fun she had enjoyed at St. Anne's when the phone rang, and we were told that my partner's wife had encountered an emotional breakdown from postpartum depression and had been taken to the hospital. We rushed to the hospital to see if we could help, but Charlie had already begun a plan for dealing with Lisa's situation and, being a take-charge kind of person, assured us that they would be fine. In essence, however, Charlie was about to go through the grieving process himself. Though Lisa would in the long term be able to attain a level of recovery which would allow them to return to a normal way of life, they had a long road ahead.

With Lisa's sudden severe health problems hitting Charlie and his family with their own version of grief, Financial Partners was on the verge of a catastrophic change. The business came to a standstill. With income being cut back, one of the things that helped the business survive was the life insurance policy that I had taken out on Cheryl and her siblings at an early age. The cash provided resources to pay final expenses and to replace income loss with the downturn in business.

When you lose a child, we found that you lose at least two years of a normal life, and what Charlie and Lisa faced going forward cost them two years of their life before they could get proper analysis of what had happened and a plan to adjust and move forward. Neither our lives nor the lives of the Hasnerls would ever be the same!

We had begun the five stages of grief after the loss of our daughter. The Hasnerls embarked on the same path after the loss of their once "normal" lives.

While both of our families embraced Christian beliefs, our faith was being challenged as never before. For both of our families, then came the question of "What's next?"

What was next for our family was more marching band competition, with the pressure on Nathan as the featured soloist going up to another level as the band prepared to compete with the ten best marching bands in the state the next Saturday.

This time, it was different. Fresh from their best-in-the-state performance in the regionals, the band took the field in the RCA Dome, the home field of the Indianapolis Colts of the National Football League, and there was no doubt that the band was ready! The band members felt it, their directors felt it, we of the field crew felt it, and the entire community felt it.

When they took the field this time, you could see, hear, and feel the confidence, and while they didn't win the state competition, they came in a very close second, which was something to celebrate. The best finish in the storied history of the Knox High School Marching Band wrapped up a week in these young people's lives that they'll never forget. It also added to our family's journey to find joy in the mourning as Nathan completed the toughest week of his life with yet *another* stellar solo performance.

The first week of grief helped us realize that life does go on and that we're not on the journey alone!

Transitioning from grief to growth can be facilitated by joining with others on the journey. Sometimes it may be difficult to find those partners with whom we can share the journey, but, oftentimes, it's as easy as looking around you at those who are already sharing other aspects of your life and, in reality, are eager to help and grow with you to find joy in the mourning!

REFLECTIONS: Chapter 6

• What was one lesson you learned in the immediate aftermath of your loss?

_____

_____

_____

_____

• What was one thing that happened in the immediate time after your loss that helped you to cope with the loss?

_____

_____

_____

_____

• How can you help others to deal with the immediate changes that take place in life after the death of a loved one?

_____

_____

_____

_____

CHAPTER 7

───────⊰◦⊱───────

GROWING THROUGH GRIEF

How will you grow through grieving? Each of us must find that path through the sixth step of grief. That sixth step, growth, is based on our own understanding of the process through which we are going.

After wrestling with my own mourning process and examining the process through the five steps of grief, I have concluded that everyone does not experience the sixth step. In fact, it can only be experienced if the person experiencing the grief *chooses* to encounter that next step. Should the griever decide to encounter that next step, it can be one which provides comfort, understanding, solace, and success in moving on in life!

In scripture, Psalm 30:5 says: "Weeping may endure for a night, but joy comes in the morning."

What I have learned in the years since we lost Cheryl is that this scripture can be used to heal the wounds of loss if we change the spelling of the word "morning" by adding the letter *u* and spell it "mourning." Yes, there can be joy in the mourning if we choose to find it.

As you go through your steps of grieving, you first need to determine if you wish to go on to the sixth step and begin to formulate a plan for your personal growth.

I have often shared the idea of finding joy in the mourning with people who have suffered such a loss. I've done it while speaking at funerals, and I've done it one-on-one with those who have had a recent loss. Invariably, the question of "How can there possibly be joy when we are mourning a loved one?" comes to those who have suffered a loss.

I usually try to answer the question before it's even asked. The answer is that you *can* find joy in mourning when you put things in perspective. This, of course, is not easy, especially in the case of a recent loss. When we suffer the loss of a loved one, we are overwhelmed with grief, and the joy we have enjoyed with them seems in the far distant past.

At most funerals today, the family usually puts pictures of the deceased on display, and the pictures often go back a long way. At funerals where I have spoken, I urge the mourners to look at the pictures on display. Invariably, those pictures show the deceased and their loved ones at gatherings where joy was being shared. Rarely have I seen pictures displayed at a funeral where the deceased and their loved ones were not smiling. So I urge the mourners to look at those pictures again and remember the joy of those moments. It's then I remind them that by remembering those happy occasions, one can indeed find joy in the mourning!

Personally, remembering the many happy and joyous moments we shared with Cheryl has more often than not pushed the shocking, painful, and negative memories to the back of my mind as I often find myself chuckling over my favorite memories of Cheryl.

The key to finding joy in mourning is to remember the good times, the fun things you did with your loved one and, yes, even thinking about what might have been! There's a mixture of sadness and joy when I think of who Cheryl would be today. I imagine what she would be doing, where she would be living, and what her family would be like.

An old country music song, "Who You'd Be Today," by Kenny Chesney, asks many of those same questions. I listen to that song often, and yes, sometimes I become very melancholy, but I often also answer the questions, and it brings a smile to my face with the answers I believe would be true!

Yes, she would have traveled the world, especially places such as Myrtle Beach, South Carolina, which she had already seen and would have loved to explore even more! Yes, she would have followed her dreams, she would have her degree in counseling and would be helping people with her work, and she probably would have owned her own counseling business.

Yes, she would have had a family one day, and she would have named her first son after her brother, Nathan, whose first comment to me after learning of Cheryl's death was "I've lost my best friend!"

————— ★ ★ ★ —————

You *can* find joy in the mourning, but you first must *look* for it!

One of the benefits of finding joy in the mourning is that when you reach that step in the grieving process, you can begin to think about using that mourning as a pathway to growth in your life!

Merriam-Webster defines growth as the process of growing: progressive development, evolution, increase, and *expansion*![15] And there are five principles of growth, as growth is

1. Continuous
2. Gradual
3. Sequential
4. Something that varies from person to person
5. A process that proceeds from general to specific[16]

Experiencing the sixth stage of grief requires an understanding of what growth is and a commitment to effect growth in your life, understanding that it can help you like nothing else in regaining your life.

To find growth, you must examine your life, your goals, your accomplishments, and your failures. In addition, you must examine what you would like to see manifest in your life. And once you determine what you want to have happen going forward, you're on your way to finding joy in the mourning!

REFLECTIONS: Chapter 7

• Who do you think your child would be today, had they lived?

_____

_____

_____

_____

• What's one way that your loss could be used for good?

_____

_____

_____

_____

• *When* will you decide to begin seeking growth in your life?

_____

_____

_____

_____

CHAPTER 8

────────── ༄ ༄ ༄ ──────────

FINDING GOOD

On the wall in our home is a plaque that Becky and I received as a wedding gift from her sister. On it is inscribed the words in scripture from the book of Romans 8:28: "[A]ll things work together for good to those who love God."

In the more than twenty-seven years that it had hung on our wall, I had read it hundreds of times, but I didn't really begin to understand what it meant until we lost Cheryl. And, even then, it took me years before I could begin to apply it to our situation.

Eventually, I came to realize that the scripture doesn't say all "good" things or all "fun" things or "all of my favorite" things: it says "all" things. Over time, I began to think that could mean challenging things, difficult things, and even bad things could work together for good.

Once that thought began to crystallize, we decided that we wanted something good to come out of the worst thing that can happen to any parent: the loss of a child!

After much thought, we decided to establish the Cheryl Lyn Welter Family Charitable Foundation in Cheryl's memory with the premise that her desire to help people could be perpetuated with the right cause.

The foundation's mission is to change the lives of underprivileged children in Indiana rural schools. That mission is pursued by collaborating with teachers and others who work with underprivileged children by providing cash grants to help them provide some of the little things . . . things which, all too often, teachers must dig into their own pockets to provide. Simple things like field trip fees, basic school supplies (which need to be replaced), and hats and gloves for wintertime are often out of reach for those underprivileged students.

We chose this as the foundation's mission for three reasons. First, the Welter family has always been involved in education. Cheryl's mom, Becky, is a retired teacher, and her mother established the first-ever kindergarten in the Knox Community School Corporation after having one in her home for many years. I served on the local school board for twenty-five years. Both of our daughters are licensed teachers: one teaches elementary school and the other is a counselor. Our son-in-law became the principal at Knox High School. So we are familiar with the challenges teachers who work with underprivileged students are faced with daily.

The second reason is that, in our research, we couldn't find anywhere in the entire state of Indiana where teachers could go to get help in supplying these little things. To be sure, there are grants available from various sources, but we found that usually these are big grants worth thousands of dollars which are offered for a single specific purpose. In addition, these grants require voluminous applications that require many hours of work for which many teachers don't have time.

Considering this knowledge, we determined that small grants which addressed needs (that could be different for each teacher) could be an effective tool to help kids who are less fortunate. Our knowledge of the needs of teachers and that a few hundred dollars in a classroom could make a substantial difference in students' lives was a key factor in choosing the mission of the foundation.

The third reason the mission to help underprivileged kids was determined to be the purpose of Cheryl's foundation was very personal to me. I had grown up outside of Knox the youngest of seven children raised by a single mom. She never got past the third grade in school, she never learned to drive a car, she was crippled by polio at an early age, and she had also lost a child who was just two days old. Yet she raised those seven children in a house which didn't have electricity, running water, or indoor plumbing, and all seven of us became productive members of society. The Welter family knows what it means to be underprivileged, and that was a deciding factor in establishing the mission of Cheryl's foundation.

The fact that I decided to take that sixth step in the grieving process, *growth*, didn't mean it would happen quickly or without drawbacks. The road to growth proved to be slow and bumpy.

The death of a child is followed by a lengthy time of pain, sorrow, and regret. In my case it was two years that, looking back, was a blur, a period of nonproductive time which seemed to drag by without being able to concentrate on the things necessary to survive. This included bouncing from one thing to another, eventually taking care of the things that absolutely had to be done to take care of client needs and keep our business running even though it wasn't growing as it had been. In my conversations with others who have had a death of a child or, as in one early case I discussed with a friend, two years seems to be the norm before any real progress can be made.

———— ⋆ ★ ⋆ ————

Finding good in a tough situation is not easy. It takes self-examination, thought, and an intense focus on what you expect out of life, going forward. Once you begin to experience the five principles of growth, however, you will be on your way to finding joy in the mourning!

REFLECTIONS: Chapter 8

• Do you have memories of your loved one that bring you joy? List three of those memories.

_____

_____

_____

_____

• Name a trait of your loved one that you would like to spread to others.

_____

_____

_____

_____

• Name one person you would like to help find joy in the mourning!

_____

_____

_____

_____

CHAPTER 9

FINDING THE RIGHT TIME

There is an old saying that "Time heals all wounds." In the case of losing a child, this saying is just not *true*.

Healing in the case of losing a child is never complete; however, finding solace for that pain can happen if you commit to taking the sixth step of grief, which is transformational growth!

Looking back, starting the foundation in Cheryl's memory seems to have been a very natural development to find growth out of grief, but it was nearly eight years before I really talked about it with anyone. I first discussed the possibility of the foundation with our daughter, Susan, who, by that time, had received a master's degree in counseling. We put some basic thought into what the foundation might look like, then began to investigate the legalities involved, even talking with an attorney whom Susan had gone to college with and who had some knowledge of the subject. Soon, however, the road seemed to be too long and complicated, so I put the idea on the back burner.

Another five years passed before I determined that we had to move forward. By then, the rules for establishing non-profits had been eased, and we were able to put together a family charitable foundation and get a designation as a 501(c)(3) organization, which would mean that donations could be tax deductible for the donors.

Over the next two years, we put together the ideas we had to establish an endowment and set the parameters of how we would operate and how grants would be awarded to help underprivileged kids. We did this with the help of a group of volunteers who served as an informal Board of directors. The group of fifteen people included schoolteachers and administrators as well as people who were community minded and had a knowledge of how the community worked. Several were friends of Cheryl or her teachers, as well as family members. The first meeting of the committee turned my thinking on its head!

Almost immediately after losing Cheryl, we had established a college scholarship in her memory to go to a deserving student from Knox High School. Using that concept in thinking about the foundation, I had assumed we would set up something to benefit Knox students through their teachers. However, the committee members had other ideas! Despite the fact that they were all tied to Knox and the Knox schools, when I brought up that the foundation's purpose was to help Knox students, I was interrupted by a committee member who suggested that we should not be so limited in our thinking. Quickly, other members professed their support for the idea of going beyond Knox to benefit kids.

"We shouldn't care where the students come from. We should be in this to help kids, not just Knox kids," one of the members stated. Another said, "We don't care if the kids we help are from Knox or Winamac or La Crosse we just want to help kids."

This concept made sense from several standpoints. Since I was going to be the point man for the foundation, my experience in working with schools all around the area, both in my profession as a financial advisor and as a sportscaster on the local radio station that covered numerous schools in a thirty-five-mile radius of Knox, made me the logical choice to work with those schools. And, by doing so, it would open a lot more opportunities for financial support as well. In the end, that concept has been one of the big keys to the success which the foundation has enjoyed.

By late 2016, we began to search for people who would support the foundation financially.

Not really knowing how to set goals, I decided that if we could get $100,000 into an endowment, we could begin awarding grants, and other donations would follow. There wasn't anything magic about that figure; it just seemed like an achievable goal. Plus, six figures seemed like it would tell a good story of how we were able to raise funds that we could then transmit to other potential donors who may be more likely to donate to an organization that obviously had already been successful.

As a financial advisor, I knew how money works and thought that a hundred thousand dollars, invested wisely, could provide a return each year which could give us a running start on awarding grants without having to always be looking for new money.

We began with $10,000 donated by our family, then we found several other people who each gave $1,000 because they believed in what we were doing. With that, the Cheryl Lyn Welter Family Charitable Foundation was off and running, and my journey through grief to growth was established as a life-changing process.

Though I didn't realize it at the time, I began to experience the five principles of growth; that is, my work in building the foundation would have to be

1. Continuous (It wasn't going to be a one-and-done effort.)

2. Gradual (It was going to take time, both to get it running and to keep it running.)

3. Sequential (The plan had to be executed with the steps in proper order.)

4. Something that varies from person to person (I had to do it my way.)

5. A process that proceeds from general to specific (It had to evolve from the conception of helping kids to the execution of a plan that would establish *how* the kids would be helped.)

———— ★ ★ ★ ————

There is no one-size-fits-all solution to finding the right time to act on our journey to growth. Taking such a step is as individual as the grieving process itself. We shouldn't purposely delay taking that first step, but we shouldn't force ourselves to take it either. Otherwise, we may get discouraged with lack of progress or take steps thinking that we have to in order to keep the growth going. The timing of the path to growth isn't as important as clearly establishing the five principles of growth in our undertakings.

REFLECTIONS: Chapter 9

• Do you feel you are ready to pursue the path to growth?

_____

_____

_____

_____

• What is the first step you will take toward an action plan to move forward?

_____

_____

_____

_____

• Whom do you know—someone who has shown growth after the loss of a child—who you can contact to ask for advice?

_____

_____

_____

_____

CHAPTER 10

LEARNING TO GROW

The experience of achieving growth through your grief is multi-faceted. By that, I mean there is more than one part to the equation of growing despite devastating grief. Being able to grow through your grief means that you're going to have to consciously *make* that decision.

I have found after making that decision, I was learning to grow in a number of areas, and, as a result, I began to understand God's plan for my life as well. Understanding God's plan is something Christians often talk about but, too often, don't really believe it's something they can ever truly understand. In reality, of course, we instinctively know that we can never understand everything, that life is an ongoing learning process. This concept even goes to the point of understanding your philosophy of faith.

One of my favorite questions to the students in my confirmation class that you may wish to ask of yourself is: "Do you believe that Heaven is a destination, or do you believe that it's a continuation of the journey of life?"

In other words, do you think that once you get to Heaven, you've experienced the true and total meaning of happiness and joy and believe that it will stay with you for all eternity? Or, on the other hand, do you believe that when you get to Heaven, you will have eternal joy.

But do you also think that you will continue to learn about God and grow closer to Him as you experience more and more of what He has prepared for you?

I tell my students that there's no right or wrong answer to that question, and whichever concept is the most valid for them, total joy is in store. It also addresses other basic questions we may have about life after death. For instance, many people, when their favorite dog dies, ask the question, "Do dogs go to Heaven?"

My brother Jim, the philosopher, often answers that question with a question: "Do you *believe* that you'll see your dog in Heaven?"

He then says that if you don't believe that you'll see your dog in Heaven, then you probably won't.

This elementary question, I believe, can be applied to our faith as a whole. If a person doesn't believe there's a God or a heaven, do you think that person will ever see either?

I've come to believe that I'll see Cheryl again in Heaven. If I didn't believe that, then it probably wouldn't happen. I believe that Cheryl lives, and I believe that because of my faith in God. And I believe she lives because I believe she has sent me subtle messages that I've received at times in my life when I needed to receive them. I'll share some of those messages later in this book.

As I've said previously, I've also come to believe that we can find growth in our grief and, as a result, understand our faith—and *ourselves*—better. Sometimes, this part of the journey is surprising, eye-opening, and also exceedingly difficult!

I think I first started to understand that we can grow through our grief if we see opportunities to take actions because of what we're going through and then *take* those actions. In my case, taking actions which would directly correspond with who Cheryl was and what her dreams were specifically pointed toward helping others. After all, she had been accepted into the Purdue University School of Child and Family Counseling. She was planning to make a career out of helping others.

The way her choice of that program at Purdue came about still makes me smile every time I remember our trip to Indianapolis together.

As our four children were growing up and getting to the point of seriously thinking about what they would do career wise, a friend suggested we take them to a career counselor he had used for his children. Since I had very limited experience in the college realm, I wasn't aware that such a service even existed, so I was prone to taking my friend's advice. I had a great deal of respect for him, both professionally and personally, as I had been a guest in his home and saw what was obviously a well-thought-out and spirit-filled family life.

The process the career counselor used was to provide students with an in-depth questionnaire of more than six hundred questions covering their academic and personal preferences along with their interests and activities.

After the questionnaire was submitted, the counselor entered the information into a computer program that helped him break down the students' interests and abilities into understandable areas. This was in the early days of the use of technology in areas such as this, so I was impressed by his approach.

One of the rules of collaborating with the counselor was that he didn't want to meet or talk with the student prior to a meeting in which he would disclose what the program told him. His advice, therefore, was given with no preconceived notions or prejudices which may have come from the personal knowledge of the student or the student's family.

When Cheryl's sister Susan took the exam, she had already been in college for a year. Her test results showed that it would likely be in her best interest to make some adjustments in her career plans, which she did. The program was partially responsible for her going in the direction of political science, which led to her taking a position on Capitol Hill in Washington, DC, rubbing shoulders with senators, congressmen, and presidents. Indeed, her experiences in Washington could fill a book in itself!

On the other hand, Cheryl's sister Laura had decided to be a schoolteacher when she was in kindergarten. The counselor's exercise confirmed her decision, and she followed through without a single doubt about her career choice.

Cheryl's situation was different, as she frequently said she had no idea what she wanted to do after graduating high school. Other than the fact that she was a people person, she gave little indication of what might appeal to her as a career, so she was anxious to take the counselor's test to see where it led her.

As we took the hundred-mile drive from our home to the counselor's office in Indianapolis, we had fun discussing the possibilities of what the test results might show. We talked and laughed about things those results might show. Could the test show that she should become a brain surgeon? No, she didn't think she'd like to stay in college for eight or ten years to achieve that goal, and, besides, she didn't like the sight of blood.

What about if the test results showed that she should become an entertainer? Yes, she'd probably like to star opposite Leonardo DiCaprio from the hit movie *Titanic*, but living in Hollywood, she said, wouldn't be her thing! The possibilities seemed to be endless.

When we arrived at the counselor's office, the wait was short before we were invited to join him for the analysis. He entered the room, sat down at his desk, and turned on a tape recorder so that we would have the conversation to review in the weeks and months ahead.

In less than a half hour, the counselor analyzed Cheryl's test results. When it was all said and done, he told Cheryl that, based on the test results, she should seek a career working with families on a personal basis, perhaps as a child and family counselor. He pointed out that the best college in Indiana for her to attend would be Purdue University, which had a School of Child and Family Counseling that was recognized for excellence all across the country.

As we drove away from the counseling session, Cheryl told me, "Dad, I think you wasted your money on this counseling session!"

I was shocked by her comment because I had thought the session had gone very well, and we had come away with some solid answers and a game plan for her college education.

"Why would you say that?" I asked.

"Dad!" she said, "the counselor didn't tell us anything we didn't already *know*!"

In retrospect, she was correct! And, as we enjoyed a leisurely dinner together and talked about it, we agreed that we knew she was already headed in that direction. With her being such a people person, given her open personality, her fun-loving, positive approach to life, and her ability to appreciate people of all persuasions, she had been leaning in this career direction all along!

"But," I told her, "I didn't waste my money, because it was worth it to get to spend the day together talking about serious as well as fun things."

Decades later, that day stands out in my mind as one of the best of my life!

———— ★ ★ ★ ————

Learning to grow through your grief can come from thinking about the past, but it also requires focusing on the future, and, most importantly, devising a plan to be effective in your life and in the lives of those around you. Once you devise that plan, you can be on your way to finding joy in the mourning.

REFLECTIONS: Chapter 10

• Name one action you will take to memorialize your lost child.

_____

_____

_____

_____

• Name one way in which you have changed since your loss.

_____

_____

_____

_____

• What's your favorite memory of you and your lost child together?

_____

_____

_____

_____

CHAPTER 11

⁊ ⊚ ⵑ

LEARNING ABOUT YOUR CHILD

Understanding that we can grow through our grief if we take actions because of what we're going through is the epitome of finding joy in the mourning. In my case, the Cheryl Lyn Welter Family Charitable Foundation directly correlates with who Cheryl was and what her dreams were, which directly pointed to helping others.

One of Cheryl's favorite high school teachers, Staci Bolakowski, describes who Cheryl was from her unique position as not only a teacher but also Cheryl's friend:

- Fun-loving
- Feisty
- Loyal
- Talented
- Beautiful

"These are the very first qualities that I think of when I reminisce about Cheryl Lyn Welter," Staci said. "It has been a challenge for me to even put those words on paper because even though she has been gone for many years, I feel like she was a student in my high school classroom just days or weeks ago. Her spirit and personality had that much effect on me.

"My first adventures with Cheryl were on her first day of Freshman Honors English at Knox High School in August of 1998. I was giving my first-day presentation about classroom rules, expectations, and course content. Cheryl was very content and determined to have an early-morning conversation with her friend Adrienne Thomas, who was sitting directly behind her. As I politely asked her to face forward and pay attention, she kept talking and gave me the common gesture for 'Wait one minute, I'm not finished.' With any other student, I believe I would have been a little sterner concerning that response. And her classmates just sat there in stunned silence as she finished her conversation. For some reason, I was not rattled or upset. I don't think I fully realized it then, but school life with Cheryl from that moment on was going to be an adventure!

"One of the blessings of being an English and journalism teacher and adviser at Knox High School for thirteen years was that I got to accompany so many students as a teacher for their entire high school careers in several classes, and Cheryl was no exception. She applied to and made it on the *Sandbur* yearbook staff as a sophomore and quickly became one of the staff's best photographers over the next two years, winning awards at the local and state levels. I also taught her in AP English her senior year. Early on in her junior year, she 'adopted' the top left-hand corner of my huge teacher's desk by taping off a rather substantial corner and dubbing it 'Cheryl's Other Locker,' complete with a sign for all to see. With her hectic class schedule, she decided it was easier to keep a stash of her schoolbooks and supplies on the second floor in my classroom instead of hiking to her assigned locker.

This practice continued into her senior year, and, over time, she also adopted a handmade cushioned stool that was in my classroom as her very own and placed it near her 'other' locker. Woe to the person who thought they could sit there when Cheryl was not around (which wasn't very often); she claimed that space as her very own.

"One of her favorite things to do when seated near my desk was to share with me and anyone who would listen to her 'deal of the day.' Those deals of the day covered an entire spectrum of topics:

"'Miss B, what is *wrong* with boys?'

"'Miss B, why do high school students have to take math classes?'

"'Miss B, do you think the cafeteria could bring back those rectangular pizzas that we used to get in elementary school? Best. Pizza. *Ever*!'

"'Miss B, *Titanic* is the most excellent movie ever made. I have seen it at the theater every day after school for the last two weeks!'

"'Miss B, boys are the *best*!'

"Every starter statement was followed up with great conversation, the occasional rush of tears, and, always, tons of laughter. I was always a little lost when Cheryl was absent or was out on a journalism assignment. Her 'deals of the day' were a highlight for her classmates and me!

"The most important thing I remember about Cheryl is her commitment to her classmates and her friends. Relationships were her life, and she was a part of the very wonderful KHS Class of 2001. They were a tight-knit group. They just had a special bond and energy when they were together, and Cheryl was a huge part of that. She did have a close circle of friends, but I can confidently say that Cheryl never knew a stranger at Knox High School. Students sitting alone in the cafeteria didn't do so for long because Cheryl did not hesitate to invite that person to join her group for lunch. She was always looking to chat someone up or make them feel included in whatever activities were happening in some way.

"That connects in a very real way to my last memory of Cheryl: coaching her class's Ironman Volleyball team with her best friend Becky and her other classmates on to victory and celebrating in the high school gym on that fateful Thursday evening of homecoming week, October 12, 2000. Everyone was a part of the fun. No one was left out.

"Cheryl's short life has made an impression on me that made me a better person and educator. The strength of her family during those days and months after her passing were inspirational and helped to strengthen my own aspirations to work more fully in ministry with youth and young adults. I am thankful every day for the light and life that Cheryl and the Welter family have brought to me and so many others over the years."

———— ★ ★ ★ ————

Of course, the foundation's work directly corresponding to Cheryl's dreams has a double meaning for me. Helping others was Cheryl's dream, and the foundation's goal of focusing on the underprivileged directly relates to my background because I can identify with being underprivileged as I grew up being raised by a single mother who had to depend on county welfare checks to survive.

My brother Jim and I often talk about what an honor I have to deliver grant checks from Cheryl's foundation to teachers to benefit underprivileged kids. As I deliver those checks, I never fail to reminisce (albeit only with myself and my brother) about how we were raised and how fortunate we were to be raised by a mother who taught us to dream about a better life, which all seven of us were able to have, despite being raised in abject poverty. I also pray for the students who will benefit from the grants, that they may have it a little better in life, and that, when they are successful adults, that they will pay it forward in recognition of what Cheryl's life and legacy did for them.

———— ★ ★ ★ ————

Learning about your child after your loss can be one of the most uplifting aspects of finding growth through your grief. It also can help you appreciate God's plan for your life and the life of your lost child. Learning more about your children, in life and in death, can help you toward finding joy in the mourning!

REFLECTIONS: Chapter 11

• Name one way in which you have changed since losing your child.

_____

_____

_____

_____

• Name one way in which you feel you have experienced growth in your life since losing your child.

_____

_____

_____

_____

• List one way you will seek growth in your life going forward.

_____

_____

_____

_____

CHAPTER 12

―――――― ❧❦❧ ――――――

THE PATH TO GROWTH

There are many routes through grief to growth. For me, the Cheryl Lyn Welter Family Charitable Foundation has provided a route that stands out as a dramatic way to give hope to others who are struggling with the loss of a child. However, I know that such an effort isn't necessarily the route to growth for others, and it certainly isn't the only route which I have taken. Some of the other routes evolved in unexpected ways.

As a Christian, I have often stated the obvious (as I have several times already in this book). But it bears repeating: God has a plan for each of us. Everything that happens is part of His plan. We can't fully understand His plan. And, for we more egotistical types, we often say, "Why couldn't He have made His plan a lot simpler and more understandable so we humans wouldn't have to go through so much to learn what the plan entails?"

Over the years, I've come to several conclusions about God. One is that He gave us free will because while He wants us all to participate in His perfect life, He wants us to *choose* to do so. God isn't forcing us to do *anything*!

I often ask the students I teach in my confirmation class at St. Thomas Aquinas Catholic Church to think about the most fun vacation they've ever had. I ask them what their favorite memories are. Invariably, the answers are "we" did this or "we" did that, which made the vacation so much fun. When I ask them who the "we" are, it usually relates to the family or friends with whom they took the vacation.

Invariably, they conclude that a big part of the reason that they enjoyed the vacation so much was they were sharing it with those they love. I then ask them to consider how God must feel when He's able to share His Kingdom with those *He* loves!

The consensus usually is that the vacation they took wouldn't have been nearly as much fun if one or more of the family members had been forced to go with the family when they didn't like the destination or the plans the parents had determined! Likewise, perhaps God wouldn't have nearly as much fun sharing His Kingdom if some of those there really didn't want to be there! Perhaps God mourns for those who choose not to join Him in the Kingdom, but He finds joy in the mourning by sharing the Kingdom with those who longed to be there with Him!

I've come to understand that growth in life can take many routes, and involve many issues, a variety of people, and a host of circumstances. I've also come to believe that beginning to understand God's plan for our lives can be an integral part of our growth. In fact, one of the most eye-opening events of my journey to find joy in the mourning came many years after Cheryl's death.

As you know, I have long taught a confirmation class at my church that primarily includes high school freshmen and sophomores. While I have structure in my teaching to make sure that the basics of the Roman Catholic Church are at the forefront, I often surprise my students by soliciting *their* understanding of the faith and scripture. The meaning of scripture, I tell them, is how that scripture fits into their lives. The reactions I get are sometimes unique and often profound. I tell them that I'm not *teaching* them about scripture: we're *learning* about it together.

This was never more truly demonstrated than during a class on Jesus's ascension into Heaven forty days after His resurrection from the grave. I reminded them that Jesus's disciples didn't want Him to leave. He had been their rock, their leader, their inspiration for spreading the good news of His resurrection. They told Him that they couldn't go on without Him. Jesus's reaction was that He *had* to go so that He could send the Holy Spirit to them. That way, they could continue His work so they could become who they were meant to be.

After I described that scene to the students, I froze! I repeated the statement to myself, and, suddenly, I realized that this was the most stunning moment I had ever experienced in my many years of teaching that class! Later, I realized it was one of the most pivotal moments of my life. I repeated the statement to the class: "Jesus said that He had to go so that His disciples could become who they were meant to be!" Then I said one of the most difficult yet agonizingly truthful comments I ever made about scripture, indeed, about faith!

"Do you think," I asked my students, "that is why Cheryl had to go, so that I could become who I was meant to be?"

You could have heard a pin drop. I didn't ask the question expecting an answer from the students. I asked the question of *myself!* I explained to the class that the thought of that being the case was absolutely overwhelming to me but that it also perfectly exemplified what we had been talking about: that scripture has its most significance when we apply it to our own lives.

Growth can be defined in a lot of ways. The growth in my faith, the growth in my desire to learn more about what scripture says to me, and the growth in empathy for those seeking joy in the mourning was furthered by that class in the basement of a little church in rural Indiana far beyond what I could ever have imagined.

Each person suffering from the loss of a child who has gone through (or is going through) the stages of grief must find for themselves how they are going to pursue growth from their experience. If you are seeking that growth, you need to have an open mind in thinking how you can pursue that growth. It must be something which is

1. Continuous (We set up Cheryl's foundation to be an ongoing enterprise.)

2. Gradual (It took us a while to determine what our goal would be.)

3. Sequential (We proceed each year with goals and activities which are similar.)

4. Something that varies from person to person (My goals and your goals won't be the same.)

5. A process that proceeds from general to specific (We established what our overall purpose would be then set about to list the steps we needed to take to get things in motion and then to maintain that purpose.)

A place to start to pursue that growth is to think of your lost child and what made that child special. Once you determine that, you can begin to dream about how your child could be honored and remembered through your efforts.

——— ★ ★ ★ ———

The routes to growth, I've learned, can take many turns, but those turns in the route can be fun to follow and fun to learn from as we seek to find joy in the mourning!

REFLECTIONS: Chapter 12

• What made your lost child special?

_____

_____

_____

_____

• Name one thing you could do differently than you have been doing that could help you to grow as a person.

_____

_____

_____

_____

• How could that one change in your life provide a tool for growth in your life and the lives of others who are dealing with the loss of a child?

_____

_____

_____

_____

CHAPTER 13

⁓ ☙ ⁓

SIGNS ALONG THE WAY

As I said earlier, as Christians, we purport to believe in certain things pertaining to our individual lives, one being that everything happens for a purpose as part of God's plan. Another is that God is present with us in every aspect of our lives, that nothing is coincidence.

One of the steps as you seek to find growth through your grief is to think of what some would call coincidences which may have occurred in relationship to your loss.

Earlier, I told the story of the letter opener which had arrived on the day we had received hundreds of cards in the mail. In addition to recognizing instances such as that for the miracles they are, we need to remember those messages for the future because they can be reminders of our faith when times get tough.

Another message came in the form of a beautiful free-hand drawing of our favorite scripture, Romans 8:28: "All things work together for good to those who love God, to those who are called to His purpose." The drawing was done by a high school student whom I would later mentor in her journey toward the sacrament of confirmation. Shortly after that, I commissioned a work of art that would combine both those signs in a keepsake wall hanging. It, along with one of my favorite pictures of Cheryl, has been prominently displayed on my office wall ever since as a constant reminder to find joy in the mourning.

Other signs were even more dramatic, one of which changed the lives of both my business partner Charlie and me. As I pointed out, following Cheryl's death, we struggled just to keep our financial services business on an even trajectory. The prospects for a hoped-for comeback dimmed as a result of decisions made by our primary source of business. We made the very tough decision to pull away from a company which I had been representing for nearly thirty years. We just didn't know what the future would hold.

As things developed, going independent was the best thing we could have done. We saw a turnaround almost immediately, and the future of the business had never looked so bright. So bright, in fact, that another "coincidence" occurred, which led to a time of exponential growth for our company. We brought on a third partner to help us with the additional business that was coming our way. Our new partner, Devan Wallen, just happened to have been one of Cheryl's dearest friends growing up!

Devan and Cheryl were such good friends that they talked constantly. Though they never had a boyfriend/girlfriend kind of relationship, they did go to the high school prom together and shared a lot of good times together. The funniest thing about their friendship occurred when they were going into the eighth grade and Devan's father, a faith-filled musician and songwriter, took a position as a music leader at a church in Canada, and the family moved a thousand miles away.

The distance didn't stop their friendship, however. They told their families that they would like to stay in touch and asked if they could call each other on Sunday nights to keep up with what was happening in their respective lives. In those days, before cell phones were widely available, both families had landlines . . . and the long-distance charges that went with them. The families decided that they could call on Sunday evenings (because long-distance rates were cheaper then), and it was agreed that the dads would take turns paying for the calls every other week. This seemed to work well and continued for nearly a year before Devan's family decided to return to Indiana because of the family ties.

Years later, after Devan became a member of our firm, we were talking about those long-distance calls, and when I commented that it wasn't too bad because it was only once a week and we controlled the length of the calls, Devan said "You *thought* we only called once a week!"

That comment still brings a smile to my face!

———— ★ ★ ★ ————

Sometimes, the signs we need to deal with grief can be hard to find, but those signs are often easy to spot if we just think about the interactions we had with our child (or with others close to the child), especially those which bring a smile to our face. And it's that smile that brings us joy in the mourning!

REFLECTIONS: Chapter 13

• Looking back, what was one "coincidence" that gave you food for thought about the loss of your child?

_____

_____

_____

_____

• Name one person who came to be more important in your life after losing your child.

_____

_____

_____

_____

• Send a thank-you note to one person who surprised you with their role in helping you after your loss.

_____

_____

_____

_____

CHAPTER 14

———— ୨ ୧୧ ୧ ————

YOU ARE NOT ALONE

If you are to take the step of finding growth through your grief, it's important to know that you are not alone, and it helps tremendously to find family, friends, and acquaintances who can join you on your journey.

Perhaps establishing Cheryl's foundation was somewhat rooted in selfishness, as it became an important part of my grieving process. Keeping Cheryl's name and purpose alive became a part of my goal in life, and I'm hoping that she will be remembered through the foundation long after I'm gone.

Somewhat sprinkled with selfishness as it may be, the fact is that the Cheryl Lyn Welter Charitable Foundation has done an immense amount of good in helping underprivileged kids in rural schools. And, if selfishness is indeed a part of the equation, it has been rewarding that I've begun to meet others who have endeavored to keep the memory of their lost children alive through philanthropic endeavors as well.

The stories of those who have lost children and gone on to the growth phase of grief are as varied as the stories of their children. When I talked with some of these parents who had lost children but gone on to find joy in the mourning, I found that each spoke in glowing terms of how their children had grown up in the years allotted to them. When I asked how they had managed to grow in their grief, they also spoke of faith in God as being the key factor in being able to grow through their grief.

As I said earlier, it took me many years to take action to make growth happen. But some of those we talked with started an action plan almost immediately to establish a heritage for their child.

When interviewing people who had lost children, I thought it important to first ask them about who their child was. This allows them to focus on their fond memories first before talking about the day and the reason that their child died.

Tim Roth was an extraordinarily successful high school football coach at Winamac High School in Indiana. We had known each other since he was a high school athlete, as I had broadcast games in which he had played.

Tim set school and conference records as he led the Winamac Warriors to an undefeated regular season and tournament championships at both the sectional and regional levels. Though the team lost at the third level of the state tournament, they ended with a record-setting 13-1 season, and his son Tyler signed to play college football the next fall. But six months after his greatest season as a coach, his son, Tyler, who was the star of the team, lost his life in an auto accident.

Tyler was a talented young man. He was a three-sport athlete, playing baseball, basketball, and football. His favorite, and the one for which he was best known, was football. In addition to his considerable athletic accomplishments, he was an honor roll student, president of the student body (certainly, a testament to his leadership abilities), and won a high school "Oscar" for his achievements in the Musical/Drama Department. Topping it all off was his glowing personality and friendliness, which endeared him to young and old alike. So it's no wonder that, years later, Tim still talks about his son with pride.

"Tyler was wise beyond his years. If Tyler wanted to do something, he wanted to do it right," Tim recalls.

"The thing I'm most proud of is his faith. Most teenage boys don't take a deep interest in their faith. Tyler took an extremely deep interest in his faith. He participated in a variety of things in addition to sports. I don't think he really ever wanted to stand out; he just wanted to be involved. But because of his involvement, he *did* stand out.

"Less than a week after giving his high school graduation speech, Tim was working at a golf course, and, on a rainy day, he got off work early to go to baseball practice. They were getting ready for round two of the sectional baseball tournament. As he was headed toward home, he pulled out to pass a car and slammed head-on into a truck loaded with heavy stone."

Tyler was obviously seriously injured, beyond what the local small-town hospital could deal with, so he was airlifted to a trauma center hospital in Ft. Wayne, Indiana, some seventy-five miles away.

Tim Roth explains what happened next:

"We went through thirty-four hours of up and down and we and down and up and down with his condition. Of course, thirty-four was his favorite number and his jersey number in football.

"My neighbor, who was a preacher, came in, and it seemed like every time Tyler took a downspin, he would say 'I think we need a prayer,' and every time he said a prayer, Tyler's vitals went up.

"You hate to say this because you don't know how God works, but I think God was allowing Tyler to live until Tyler's cousin, who was his best friend, showed up. We then had to decide about whether to take him off life support.

"The trauma doctor was so upset he couldn't stand to tell us, so he sent someone else into the room to tell us that we wouldn't have to make the decision because Tyler had already made it, and he was gone.

"I was so mad at God. When I was nine years old, I lost my dad. Mom raised us four kids. When we got Tyler, I was ecstatic. When he died, I was mad at the world for a period of time. My priest finally helped me to understand that God's plan wasn't our plan.

"I think I got back on track much faster than the rest of the family. I went through that period, and I had to get back to doing something.

"Tyler's accident was on May 31, our son-in-law's birthday. He died on June 1. When we went to the funeral home to make arrangements, the funeral director suggested the funeral should be held on June 5 or 6. Melinda and I had been married on June 5 twenty-five years earlier, but I said it wouldn't be on June 6 because that was his mom's birthday, and I didn't want that to be the memory of her birthday until the end of time. So we buried Tyler on our twenty-fifth wedding anniversary.

"By the end of summer, it was time for football practice to start, and I didn't know if I was going to continue to coach. A number of my assistant caches came to me and said I had to do what I had to do, then one of them said that Tyler wouldn't want me to quit. That hit me right between the eyes, and I realized I had to go back.

"In football, when you get knocked down you have to get back up, and we got knocked down to the lowest of the low that you can go.

"Losing a child is just a total knockdown of who you are and what you are doing. 'Why is this happening to me?' you ask. It's a real wakeup call of 'get your stuff together and become a better person!'

"I think Melinda and I both have tried to be just that, be a better person. We might have had views before losing Tyler that have since changed. We have since realized that what we thought was important before wasn't important at all. We came to more of a conclusion that even pertaining to those we don't agree with, I can say, "Okay, God, I get it: we're all your children, and we all should get along!"

"The problem in the world today is we're not good to people and not helping them to feel better, do better, and be better."

The family has done many things in memory of Tyler which have positively affected people and the Winamac community that he loved.

"In his memory," Tim explains, "the church did a fundraiser and, in 4-H, they put his pig in the auction. A group of buyers paid nearly $10,000 for that pig, which allowed us to make a donation back to the 4-H to buy new equipment and remodel the horse arena. We also created a scholarship in Tyler's name at Winamac High School.

"When Ted Hayes at WKVI Radio asked if they could use Tyler's name for a special weekly award, we were so humbled by that. We listen to the radio every Saturday morning to find out who was the "Tyler Roth/WKVI Athlete of the Week." And being involved in the "Tyler Roth/WKVI Athlete of the Year" has been a special blessing.

"Tyler's name is also on the Indiana North-South All-Star Team Most Valuable Player Award when that game is played each summer.

"When I think of my favorite memories of Tyler, one was when he was probably three or four, and the girls were taking swimming lessons. At the end of the practice, they would have a free-swim time. So, one day, I got in the pool with Tyler, and he got on my back, and they had these rings they would throw into the pool. I would dive down, and he would get off my back and pick up those rings. Then, we'd swim back to the surface, and he would be so excited!

"Of course, there's so many football memories, especially his senior year when he had such a great season, and he led the team to a 13-1 record.

"Losing a child is the worst thing you can go through in life. It's worse than cancer, which I survived twice."

By doing positive things in Tyler's memory, Tim and Melinda Roth have found joy in the mourning!

———— ⋆ ⋆ ⋆ ————

As the Roth family saw, finding out that they were not alone in their grief and their struggles, and being encouraged by others on the journey to do positive things in Tyler's memory has helped them. Those kinds of things can help you, too, as you seek to find joy in the mourning!

REFLECTIONS: Chapter 14

• Name one person who you know who has shown growth after losing a child.

_____

_____

_____

_____

• Send an email or call that person and ask where they found the strength to grow, considering their loss.

_____

_____

_____

_____

• Describe in one sentence if faith has helped you and how.

_____

_____

_____

_____

CHAPTER 15

───── ༭ ☙ ༭ ─────

AWARENESS

Dealing with grief is an individual challenge. Perhaps your child died instantaneously, like ours did, in an auto accident. Perhaps you had some time of anticipating the death, such as the Roth family did, but others have had multiple losses, and some have had anticipatory grief for many years before their child died.

As Doug Manning, grief counselor, pastor, and author, writes, "[T]hey all hurt as much as they can."[17]

Jo Fisher lost two sons. Josh was killed in an auto accident in 2004 at the age of sixteen. An outstanding three-sport athlete, he hoped to play football and baseball at the University of Miami.

His mom explains, "He was 6'8" and 290 pounds. He donated a lot of time and volunteered at the Boys and Girls Club. He coached young kids in baseball and helped his younger brothers. He wanted to go into social work. Benjamin was three years younger, and he was in the accident which took Josh's life. Doctors told me that night that he was never going to be able to survive. The doctors said they couldn't fix it, so I turned it over to God.

When he woke up before doctors thought he would after being brought out of an induced coma, he said 'Where's my mom? Tell her to bring tacos!' It was as if he was more intelligent after the accident and the head injury. God totally healed him and gave him additional purpose in his life.

"Granted, he had a rough time over the next fifteen years without his brother there, but he did some extraordinary things. At sixteen, he started a lawn care business. He wanted to be a motivational speaker, so he just started talking with people at random, and his faith got him through. He motivated people with his positive attitude, and he testified about his faith.

"His motivation carried through to his regular workdays as well," she continued. "He always said, 'You go to work prepared daily, and you know that you're going to meet someone that day who is going to help you excel and succeed.'"

———— ★ ★ ★ ————

But the story doesn't end there.

Fifteen years after Josh died in an auto accident, his brother Ben was killed while working for a traffic control company that provided road signs and barriers in highway construction zones. A truck, going too fast, hit him when he was in a work zone.

After Ben's death, his mother began a campaign to make people aware of the dangers in highway work zones. Her work has spread all over Indiana through billboards and bumper stickers, reminding people to slow down.

When asked what inside of her has allowed her to do things like the work zone safety campaign, she said, "The Holy Spirit. Without Him, none of this would be possible.

"Benjamin and I had talked about starting a foundation and doing something about work-zone awareness," she continued, "so this was a natural follow-through."

A step to consider in your striving for growth from your grief is to determine what was important to your child and to think in terms of what you can do to further what they wanted to do.

——— ＊ ＊ ＊ ———

Anticipatory grief presents a far different challenge to parents, as Al and Sharon Breyfogle learned. They lost their son, Brad, after nine years of dealing with medical problems, then, two years later, Al lost his wife, Sharon. He tells the story of losing his only son like this:

"Brad was in his thirties the day we got a call from where he was working in Valparaiso, Indiana, and he was having difficulty breathing. At the hospital, they found a tumor, and when they tried to deal with the tumor, they accidentally severed a nerve that controls the digestive system. That started our odyssey. Once they got the tests done, they gave him four years to live and said anything longer than that would be a miracle.

Well, he lived almost nine years. We took him to all the best medical places in the country. We went to Mayo Clinic, the Cleveland Clinic, Northwestern University, the University of Chicago, and the University of Michigan.

"Brad couldn't eat; he had his stomach removed, along with most of his intestines. He had at least eighty surgeries over the next nine years.

"Of course, there were lawsuits involved. The attorneys did a report on a day in the life of Brad Breyfogle. He was nourished through a port in his chest for almost nine years, and as the attorneys learned more about how the severed nerve affected his day-to-day life, they shared it in court, in heartbreaking detail. From my perspective, among other things, I couldn't ask my son to go out to dinner anymore; I couldn't ask him to go golfing or fishing, things we both loved.

"The thing about it that made me who I am today is this: I always tell people you want to be an example to your children and show them what it is to be faithful and trust in God and to be good and giving. I went from being a teacher to being a student. I learned more from my son, especially the last four years, than from anyone else in my life as far as giving, trusting, and not being bitter.

"The only time through this whole situation was the one night he called me and said, 'Dad, I've about had it!' This was about three years before he passed away, and I told him, 'I'll be right up.'

"So we talked about it. We talked about God allowing things to happen, not *causing* things to happen. He said, 'There has to be a purpose in what happened to me! But, right now, I'm a little mad at God! It bothers me that I'm mad at Him.'

"I told him that it was okay. God gives us emotions and He understands."

"Brad said, 'I could just scream!'"

"I said, 'Let's do it!'"

"So we went out in the backyard at 10:30 at night, and we just started screaming! The lights in the neighborhood started flicking on, and people asked what we were doing.

"We said, 'We're screaming!' And one of the neighbors asked if she could scream with us! We

103

screamed at God to ask what the purpose of what Brad was going through. It did us all a world of good.

"At that point, Brad changed a little bit. He had always been a giving person. He said, 'If I could set an example and help people, and people see me in my condition helping, maybe it'll make them help more! I have to turn it. I can't just receive; I have to give.'

"The town had a benefit for him in Winamac, Indiana. They had a pork chop dinner and raised almost $25,000. He was amazed. He didn't realize he was affecting people. That was another turning point.

"He always cared about the kids. His wife worked while he took care of the kids.

"He would go to as many of his son's high school football games as he could, and when it came to Senior Night, he said he wanted to be there for his son. But there was one caveat: He wanted to *walk* down the track; he didn't want to be in a wheelchair. He had to show his son, Gavin, that he wouldn't give up.

"That year, on November 13, we had a family gathering where relatives, some he hadn't seen in a couple of years, made it a great get-together. But, afterward, he took a turn for the worse and was taken to the hospital. It had been a wonderful day of sunshine with friends and family.

"At the hospital, he was on a ventilator, but I told them, no, Brad wouldn't want that. So they took it off and he passed away.

"After those nine years of what we had been through, when he did pass, his mom, Sharon, and I responded differently. We had gotten some good advice from friends who had lost children and who told us that we would manage it differently. Some days, I would be having a bad day, and Sharon would have a good day. Other days, it would be the opposite, and we had to learn to support each other with that knowledge to keep our marriage on a positive level.

"After nine years, you think you're prepared for the end, but you're not.

"After the funeral, we wanted to make sure that Brad's name didn't get buried with Brad, because he had done too much work. He had done too much giving; he had fought too hard for him to just be gone. I could *feel* his legacy.

"After about six months, Sharon came up with the idea of 'Bradsgiving.' We just started collecting things that we would start giving. The first year, we delivered thirty-five backpacks filled with things that the homeless could use, and we took them to the homeless shelter in South Bend. Another year, we filled backpacks and went to Indianapolis and just handed them out to homeless people.

"Another time, we sponsored individual families who needed help with foster children. We've played Santa Claus to make sure needy families have a good Christmas.

"In the span of five years, I lost my only son, my only brother, and my only wife."

When I asked about him going through the sixth step of grief, growth, Al

said, "I have lost two great examples of how to handle life and how to help people!

"As a family, if we just sit around and mourn and grieve, every one of us is going to continue to suffer. The only way to lift people up is for you to get above them and then bring them up with you.

"There were times when we first started that we struggled a little bit, but that's where the faith kicked in. If you need a little extra strength, just ask God for the strength; ask Him for the guidance, ask Him for the direction. Sometimes, we didn't know the direction we were going, what we were going to do that year. And God has always given us whatever we need to do without fail. The Bradsgiving idea, since we lost Sharon, is now the Breyfogle family.

"There's nothing better than giving. One Christmas, we visited a family with three foster children, all of them suffering from disabilities, and a couple were severely disabled. The ironic thing was that we waited until after Christmas, and when I knocked on the door of the family, a Winamac graduate answered the door. A kid that I had coached in football opened that door, and he and his wife were raising these three kids with disabilities. You talk about two guys bawling like babies! We hugged each other and cried and cried. He said it made their kids' day when we brought the Christmas gifts to them. It was a classic example of God at work.

"I've found so much joy in just giving and helping people who need help. And it all started with twenty-five cents in downtown Chicago.

"Even though he had been in the hospital for days and days and was sick beyond belief, Brad had us stop to give a cup of coffee to a homeless person sitting on the sidewalk! And so, it becomes part of your life. It's not me; it's about having Brad not being forgotten . . . doing good like he always did.

"Giving now is like a snowball. Once you get in the habit of giving, it affects you. And, since losing both my son and my wife in an abbreviated period of time, I don't think there's a better way to honor them than giving.

"Everybody has the ability to give. It doesn't take a lot of talent; it doesn't take a lot of money. It only takes some time and some effort, but you'll be surprised how much it'll change your life."

———— ★ ★ ★ ————

When your child had already begun to be a giver before you lost them, it may make the way forward to continue their plans and dreams so obvious that the transition can be simple.

Drew Shearin was twelve years old, and it was Christmas morning. He was hoping that there was an electric guitar hidden somewhere in the house because he didn't see any package under the tree that looked even remotely close to resembling a guitar.

The months leading up to Christmas morning had been filled with Drew repeatedly begging his parents for a guitar, but he knew that because of the large family of which he was a part, this special request could be out of reach.

Drew had already begun to play other instruments but felt he could express his musical talents through an electric guitar more effectively. When he reluctantly turned to his final gift, he saw it was in a clothes box. He put on his best forced smile and opened the package. In it weren't any clothes, though: it was a single guitar pick.

Confused, he turned to ask his mom what this was all about. When he turned around, his mom stood there with a bright red electric guitar in her hands. Fighting back tears, which just wouldn't be cool for a twelve-year-old, he silently put it in his hands, rubbed the tears from his eyes while hugging his mom, then retreated to his room.

By late that morning, he was performing a song for the whole family, which he called "The Storm Song." It was Drew's first step toward becoming an accomplished composer by the age of sixteen.

Drew had a dream of hearing a band play his music and perform his compositions. By his second year of high school, the dream came true after one of his compositions won first place in the Indiana Music Educators Association (IMEA) state competition. Shortly thereafter, the competition chairman asked Drew to attend one of his own band's performances, where they played his concert piece called "Uncertainty."

Later that year, the musical phenom entered another IMEA competition, and his new piece won first place in the choral division of the competition. But before the Butler University Chorale performed it, Drew was killed in a single-car accident while going home from his job at a local fast-food restaurant. The cause of the accident was never determined.

Drew's family knew very quickly that they wanted to continue Drew's love of music in some fashion, and, within months, they created Drew's Gift of Music Foundation. The foundation focuses on helping students obtain and play musical instruments and participate in cultural events.

Drew's mom, Deb Johnson, explains how she was able to find the strength to carry Drew's love of music forward:

"On October 10, 2011, at 9:48 p.m., my son died in a single-car accident. When I arrived at the scene, my prayers were pleading prayers that my son was not the one in the car. Half my heart went with Drew when my prayers were not answered. Life as I knew it ended, and darkness covered everything. Days became weeks, and still no sign of hope or light could I see.

I returned to work, hoping that some sort of normal may exist. I was walking blindly through the rubble of what was left of my life and my family. Only when I could not stand anymore did I go to my knees; my plea for the Lord now became a simple request. 'Dear Father, please give me the faith that there is just a hope of light somewhere in this darkness.'

"Can I say that everything became light all at once? No! Yet I held on to the promise of that plea. I knew I had to be a part of finding that light, and I set out to find it. My biggest loneliness was the silence that enveloped my home when my seventeen-year-old gifted musician/composer was gone. I no longer could take care of Drew, but I made a promise to him that I would keep his name alive.

"God gave Drew a gift of music; Drew gave that gift of music back to anyone who wanted to hear it. I sat down with my husband and surviving children with this thought. So my journey began led by the gift given to my son, the gift of music. Drew's Gift of Music was founded in January 2012, just three months after we lost Drew.

"We drew up a mission statement that says: 'The mission of Drew's Gift of Music is to carry on Drew Shearin's passion and dedication for music and all of its arrangements by empowering students to obtain musical instruments, financial support for instruction, and scholarships for advanced music education.'

"As a grieving mother, I quickly learned speaking of my dead son often made people feel uncomfortable, yet speaking my son's name in relationship to the foundation did not seem to have the same effect. I got to speak of his music and his dreams of composing, teaching, and playing his music.

"In 2013, the foundation gave its first instrument to a student who could not afford it. Seeing the students' and parents' joy of being able to be a part of music programs made my heart leap. I got to see Drew's love grow into something great.

"Throughout my journey, I have learned what acceptance is in the loss of my son. To me, acceptance is the realization that I will carry half a heart the rest of my life. Faith will give me the strength to go on. I feel that my prayer was answered. There *is* light, even with the pain I will carry until the day I hold him in my arms again.

"I've learned that you can live a great life with half a heart. God's promise was 'All things work together for good to those who love God' (Rom. 8:28). We have tried to make sure that even this bad thing works for *good*!"

———— ★ ★ ★ ————

Whether your child died quickly or lingered, whether you've lost one child or more, the journey takes the same steps, and it begins by thinking about and getting to know your child and what they represent. In the end, faith, family, and friends can help you find direction for your growth and find joy in the mourning!

REFLECTIONS: Chapter 15

• In one sentence, describe who your child was.

_____

_____

_____

_____

• Ask someone who knew your child to write a sentence describing who your child was to them.

_____

_____

_____

_____

• Name two things you could give someone that would convey who your child was to someone else.

_____

_____

_____

_____

CHAPTER 16

PARTNERS ON THE JOURNEY

While grief is individual, partly because children die in many different ways, sometimes those in grief can find common ground with other mourners. Such was the case of two women who lived about a half hour away from each other but who never met until each had lost a son in the same manner, that is, due to heart failure while they were high school athletes.

Julie West lost her son, Jake, while he was in high school. She explains that her journey to find joy in the mourning started immediately after he died.

"Jake was a vibrant, happy kid who was smiling all the time. He had a big heart. He was just a thoughtful young man," she said.

"He was at football practice, and they went through a play, and he collapsed soon after that play. His heart stopped.

"Immediately, I felt a pain, one I feel to this day, that I can't explain. Only another parent who has lost a child could know what that feels like. I remember being in the emergency room and I remember begging out loud, 'Please save him . . . *please.*' I was talking to all in the people in the ER who were working on him, but I was also talking to God. I remember begging God to keep him here, no matter what condition he was in, saying, 'I don't care if he doesn't walk again or doesn't speak again;

I just want him here. Let me be able to hug him, to speak to him. Let me tell him that I love him.'

"Growth through grief is a choice. It's a choice I have to make every single day. I couldn't read enough after losing Jake. I couldn't pray enough. I had to somehow make sense of what happened. I had to really see how I was going to get through this. I learned that through prayer and my belief in God, He was going to help me get through it.

"I asked myself, 'What would Jake want me to do?' He and I had a really strong mother/son bond. He was always the one making me smile and lifting me up. So I try to be myself. I think if I carry that heaviness, that burden, with me around other people I care about and love, it's harder on them. So choosing growth and joy is a choice.

"In the first couple of weeks after we lost Jake, we came to find out after the autopsy that he had a preexisting heart condition. I learned that there had to be other kids out there with the same diagnosis, and we had to figure something out to help them.

"I ended up going to a heart screening at Chicago Hope Academy. I learned how to do the tests, how to put the electrodes to the heart, just months after losing Jake. I left that day, driving home in tears and exhausted, and I thought, *This is what we need to do. We need to form a foundation to do heart screenings.*

"So we formed the Play for Jake Foundation, and we went into schools and did heart screenings. We lost Jake in September and started this in January.

"A lot of times, there are no symptoms. The screenings reveal the condition of a child's heart. Within two months, we found our daughter, who was two years older than Jake, also had a heart condition. Her brother saved her life!

"I was told that I needed to get screened, but I was in my grief, and my mother came to me and said, 'Julie, you just go and do it *now*!' So I did. I listened to my mother, and they found that I had a condition which could take my life at any time. I didn't have any symptoms.

"I found another mother who had lost a child with this condition, Teresa Mago, who started the Zac Mago Foundation, and now we work together with Play Heart Smart from Indianapolis to give heart screenings and to spread the word all over the state."

— ★ ★ ★ —

Teresa Mago lost her son at age seventeen between his junior and senior years of high school. She explains who Zac Mago was like this:

"Zac was a friend to everyone and was especially concerned about the underdogs in any situation. He was our child with the most potential, he said, after we were on an airline flight and the attendant, when going through the emergency procedures, said that parents should put their own oxygen mask on and then begin helping the children, starting with the one with the most potential and he said, "Mom, that's *me*!" Anything he set his mind to, he would do!

"I was away from home with my sister for the afternoon when he passed away. He had gone to take a nap, saying he didn't feel good. I got home, and a little later, his sister went upstairs to wake him up since he had to get ready to go to Indianapolis the next day for a basketball camp. She tried to wake him several times, then rolled him over, and I heard her scream, 'Call 911!!'

"We tried applying CPR, but he was already gone.

"What I remember after the emergency response team had come and tried to revive him was that a lot of people came to the house, and we had a lot of support from friends and family. But it's such a blur.

"We didn't find out what had taken him until late August, nearly two months after he had died in early July. It was a heart condition that took him.

"He had had a heart screening when he was fourteen, but I found out six months later that heart screenings should be done more frequently than that with growing kids. When I found that out, I knew what we would do. We would do heart screenings.

"We started the Zac Mago Foundation to do those screenings, and we did our first heart screening in May, less than nine months after we lost Zac. Our first heart screening found a young man who had a heart condition, so that was the first life we saved as a result of our efforts.

"We realized that if Zac had had another heart screening, our lives might be different.

"We had our first fundraiser for the foundation, and one of our supporters started talking about the importance of having automated external defibrillators (AEDs) available in various venues, so we started to fundraise to get AEDs placed in schools, at practice facilities, and so forth.

"We were doing the heart screenings, then COVID came along and put everything on hold, but then I said that we had to resume the screenings because more young people could die of a heart condition than from the virus!

"So I learned of others who were interested in the same things that our foundation is doing. I found Play Heart Smart in Indianapolis and, of course, Julie West in LaPorte, and we work together. We aren't formally joined, but we work closely to ensure we can reach as many young people as possible.

"If I didn't move forward, and I just stayed stuck, I feel like Satan would win, and I couldn't let that happen. I had a powerful dream where Zac appeared to me and told me how beautiful Heaven is and how much he loves me . . . and I knew I had to go on. I reread a drawing from one of my kid's birthday parties that hangs on my refrigerator. It says, 'Today Is a Good Day for a Good Day!' and that's been my motto. If I have a bad day, I change it to 'Tomorrow Is a Good Day for a Good Day!'

"You can't go back; he's not coming back. So I look to the future, knowing that I'll see him again. The grief never goes away, it just gets different, allowing us to move forward and grow.

———— ★ ★ ★ ————

When it comes to losing a child, age makes no difference. It matters not whether the loss is a newborn, a teenager or a grown-up, the loss is like no other.

———— ★ ★ ★ ————

Finding others who have lost children can be part of the growing aspect of grief. And if you can find common grounds on which you can share your grief with one another, and especially if that sharing can lead to working together to help others, you can, together, begin to find joy in the mourning!

REFLECTIONS: Chapter 16

• Name one person who you know who has shown growth after losing a child.

_____

_____

_____

_____

• Send an email or call that person and ask where they found the strength to grow, considering their loss.

_____

_____

_____

_____

• Describe in one sentence if faith has helped you and the role it has (or has *not*) played in your journey toward growth.

_____

_____

_____

_____

CHAPTER 17

AGE MAKES NO DIFFERENCE

When parents lose a child, the circumstances don't matter, and age makes no difference.

My friend Shirley Young-Walters was pregnant for the first time after four and a half years of using fertility treatments and praying for a miracle. She and her husband, Rick, learned that they would not only have a baby but triplets!

The joy faded when Shirley went into labor at twenty-four weeks. Two of the babies were stillborn; the third, Kazia Ann, lived for twenty days but remained in isolation most of that time. Her parents held her only once, and that was as she was dying. Those twenty days have been remembered all these years since.

After the loss, Shirley was asked to tell her story to help another friend going through something similar.

"I reluctantly agreed," Shirley says. "It was very painful to write, and I wrote it with tears in my eyes."

But Shirley found that this experience was the beginning of finding good feelings by giving to others.

Shirley became a professional photographer, both as a photojournalist and as a personal photographer. As such, she had many opportunities to photograph memorable events in the lives of young people and their families. After losing her triplets, she began to think more and more about the importance of families and their experiences and found that many people appreciated the picture stories she was able to capture at important family moments.

Oftentimes, her photographs were of high school sporting events, capturing important moments in games for the local newspaper, but she also shared them with family members. Their appreciation for her photos continues through the entire lives of those whose endeavors she was able to capture on film.

Over time, Shirley's understanding of the frailty of life brought on by the loss of their children led her to help others understand the value of pictures to remember loved ones. In addition, Shirley and Rick got involved in other activities around schools; in particular, she served as a substitute teacher for many years, some of them as their other children went through school themselves.

Shirley and Rick Walters grew through their loss by getting involved in helping others understand the beauty of life, no matter how long it is. They were amazed, fifteen years after the loss of their triplets, when they found they were expecting twins. While one was lost to miscarriage, their first son survived and would be joined later by two more siblings.

Shirley and Rick used their faith and their own efforts of helping others to begin finding joy in the mourning!

— ★ ★ ★ —

Kim Werner loved teaching, which she did at South Central High School, her alma mater, from the time she got her teaching degree. I first met her when she was in high school in my role as a radio sportscaster covering area high school games. When she returned as a teacher and coach, she was frequently my guest for radio interviews discussing her various teams' activities. Our mutual love of high school sports led to an enduring friendship, which was capped by a conversation we had at a fundraising event for the Cheryl Lyn Welter Charitable Foundation. During that talk, we discussed various ways in which students at area schools had raised funds for the foundation. She decided that when school started that fall, she would get her students involved with the foundation and its work. Though nothing definite was planned, we both understood that once things died down after the rush of the opening weeks of school that fall, we would get together and devise a plan.

Before we talked further, Kim died unexpectedly at the age of fifty-three. When her parents learned about what Kim was planning to do with the foundation, they asked folks who wanted to honor Kim to make a contribution to Cheryl's foundation instead of sending flowers. They raised over $6,500 to help the foundation, a big shot in the arm at that time in our development. In addition, the family became regular donors themselves. This was their positive response in seeking to continue their daughter's lifelong work of helping young people. They've used this as a vehicle to continue to find joy in the mourning.

In my own family, as I've mentioned, my mother lost a child at two days old. That preceded my birth two years later. Looking back, my mother never stopped grieving, but she always reminded all of us to remember our sister Jeannette!

In addition, just ten months before we lost Cheryl, our niece, Bernadette Manuel, lost her two-year-old son when he wasn't being watched closely and drowned in a backyard children's swimming pool. He lay on life support for several months before passing.

Having lost her own mother at an early age, Bernadette struggled to deal with the loss of her son. But she found a way as she experienced growth, both as a parent and in her professional life, by eventually becoming an elected county official who was recognized all over the state of Indiana by other political officials as being the very best at what she did.

Whether the child you lost was two days old, twenty days old, or fifty-three years old when death comes knocking, the challenge of finding growth through grief needs to be your focus.

———— ★ ★ ★ ————

When it comes to losing a child, age makes no difference whether they're grown children or they're young. Coming to grips with the loss and finding ways to help others in the process can help parents find joy in the mourning!

REFLECTIONS: Chapter 17

- How old was your child when you lost them?

_____

_____

_____

_____

- How would you have celebrated their next birthday?

_____

_____

_____

_____

- What can you do to celebrate their next birthday in a way that can help others?

_____

_____

_____

_____

CHAPTER 18

———— ༚ ༀ ༚ ————

HELPING OTHERS

There's no question that a big step for me to find growth through the grief of losing Cheryl was finding that I could help others who had comparable stories to tell about their struggles to work through their grief.

We talked earlier about Su Clark's visit to Cheryl's wake to bring us comfort. With her visit, Su set a splendid example. The whole purpose of her visit was not to give advice but to give hugs and a shoulder to cry on, to assure us that we were not alone in our grief and to let us know that there were people who could understand what we were going through.

Our first opportunity to do for others what Su Clark did for us came just seven months later.

When Tyler Roth lost his life in a head-on collision, I received notice of the accident from a mutual friend of Tyler's father, Hank Orkis. Hank and I were longtime friends from my radio broadcasting career, so he knew that I would want to know about the Roths' situation.

Within a few hours, I talked with Tim Roth on the phone about the accident and Tyler's condition. He told me that things did not look good because Tyler had suffered brain injuries and other injuries, but that they would know more within twenty-four hours.

Late the next evening, we learned that Tyler had died from his injuries.

Taking a cue from Su Clark's visit to us following Cheryl's death, Becky and I, along with our daughter Laura, and son, Nathan, drove to the Roths' home early the next morning.

As we arrived at the Roths' home, we learned that Tim and his wife, Melinda, were taking a walk. Their daughter welcomed us into the house, and we waited for a few minutes before they returned from the walk. They seemed almost shocked that we were there. It was their first realization that they were not alone in their grief. Just as Su Clark had simply shown that she understood without offering advice, we simply provided a presence which we believed spoke for itself. While Tim and I had been friends for many years, following our visit, the friendship took on a new meaning, one on which we have built for these many years since.

— ★ ★ ★ —

Helping others is something which has played a big part in the grieving process for me, and that includes helping others through the Cheryl Lyn Welter Charitable Foundation.

Some of the stories from those who have received grants from the foundation signal that Cheryl's life goal of helping others is being actualized. Teachers have used the grants in many different ways, from providing playground additions to benefit students who are physically challenged to supplying food baskets to students whose families are unable to afford adequate nutrition for their children over the weekends. Other teachers have used grants to provide items such as special glasses for colorblind students to enhance their enjoyment of art class and field trip fees to students who couldn't otherwise afford them,

In the appendix, you can learn how Cheryl's foundation grants have changed lives.

———— ★ ★ ★ ————

Finding ways to help others who are dealing with a loss like yours can help you on your own journey and help others to do the same. Seeing the results of sharing who your child was with others in ways that help them can be a big step in finding joy in the mourning!

REFLECTIONS: Chapter 18

• Name one person who you know who has also lost a child.

_____

_____

_____

_____

• Write a note of encouragement to that person.

_____

_____

_____

_____

• Make a list of everyone you know who has lost a child who you could talk with at a later time.

_____

_____

_____

_____

CHAPTER 19

REMEMBERING THE GOOD TIMES

One of the biggest keys to finding joy in the mourning is remembering the good times, the fun times spent with your child before they were taken.

My favorite memory of spending time with Cheryl came a matter of weeks before she was killed. It was a beautiful Sunday in August, and Cheryl wanted to go to a mall to shop. It was a last-minute kind of decision on her part, and she began calling some of her friends who might want to go along. But the mall she had in mind was in Merrillville, Indiana, nearly an hour away.

On such late notice, none of the friends she contacted could go with her, so, as a last resort, she asked me if I would accompany her. I wasn't necessarily thrilled to be going shopping, but since the two of us never seemed to have a lot of one-on-one time together, I thought it might provide some good father/daughter time together, so I agreed to drive her up there.

Arriving at the mall, I told her to shop to her heart's content and, when she was finished, to come and get me. I would be in the bookstore, I told her (since that was about the only place in *any* mall at which I cared to shop).

As she headed through the mall, I turned into the bookstore and quickly found the history section and began reviewing books. In less than five minutes, Cheryl was standing by my side.

127

"Dad, it's no fun to shop alone!" she said. "Come with me!"

So I dutifully began to tag along.

While I was initially less than thrilled to be moving from one teenybopper shop to another, I quickly began to enjoy it when I saw Cheryl's excitement as she found things she really liked and just *had* to try on. As she tried on one outfit after another and modeled each one for my approval, I really got caught up in the moment as we laughed and joked about some of the clothes that, for one reason or another, just weren't "her." I know she tried on several knowing that I wouldn't like them, but she got a kick out of seeing my reaction.

After a couple of hours of bouncing around the mall, something happened that left us laughing hysterically. We went into a teen dress shop, and she found an outfit she really liked and went into the changing room to try it on. I walked over toward the checkout line because I had a suspicion that this was going to be one of the items I'd be buying for her.

As I looked behind the checkout desk, I stopped in my tracks. The young girl who was behind the cash register looked exactly like one of Cheryl's best friends. By that, I mean she could have been her *twin*!

When Cheryl came out of the dressing room wearing what was soon to be her newest outfit, she twirled around to get my approval. I smiled and told her I thought it looked perfect on her. I then quietly told her to slowly turn around and inconspicuously look behind the checkout counter. When she did so, she turned back to me with eyes as big as saucers.

"Oh, my gosh!" she exclaimed, "She looks like Carrie's twin!"

Of course, that's what I was thinking and said, "Wow! Cloning must be real!"

We began to laugh and continued to do so as Cheryl went back to the dressing room to change. In fact, we laughed about that the rest of the day!

After having lunch and doing some last-minute browsing, our drive home was filled with conversation about her senior year, which was now underway. It was the last extensive one-on-one time we ever had. As such, it's a day which I relive frequently because it gives me, even after all these years, joy in the mourning!

If you don't know how to start on the journey to growth after losing your child, I believe that a good place to begin is to choose your most favorite memory of the time you spent with your child. Remember *everything* about that time. Writing down your memories might help. You may find that you know your child better after focusing on those favorite memories than you did when your child was with you. Now, that isn't a negative, but it is the truth because most of us, when we were raising our children, didn't have the time or energy to spend on focusing on each little detail of something we had done together. But when you know there'll be no more moments like that ever again, you focus on every detail you can remember, no matter how minor it may seem, and you appreciate those moments like you would never have been able to if your child was still with you.

We have found joy in the mourning because we have had partners on the journey. Cheryl affected everyone she met in such a positive way that, even decades later, her friends can relate stories of their friendships as if they happened last week.

Becky Vollmer Johnson was Cheryl's longest-standing best friend and remembers the fun they had growing up and how Cheryl affected others.

"While Cheryl was a friend to all, I was the luckiest; I got to call her my best friend. It was a friendship that started when we were three, and it grew with each passing year, but it became the strongest during those defining high school years. We bonded over what most high school girls bond over . . . boys, sports, and classes . . . oh, and did I mention *boys*? We saw each other through some sweet, new relationships and were each other's shoulders to cry on through teenage heartbreak. We spent countless hours talking on the phone about what can only be described as "girl talk." The many days and nights spent together turned our friendship into family. Mr. and Mrs. Welter became a thing of the past . . . it was Mom and Dad Welter from then on in."

Becky tells the story about how Cheryl talked her into going out for the high school golf team because the coach had "beautiful blue eyes," and although neither had played a lot of golf, they had a fun season traveling with Coach Kelly Shepherd and their teammates to tournaments all around Northern Indiana.

Becky also noted that Cheryl was friendly to everyone and, although she could kid most anyone, it was never malicious. She also said that Cheryl could make friends with anyone but never at the expense of lifelong friendships such as they had built since the age of three. Her group of friends simply grew as Cheryl felt other people needed to be included.

Allison Smith Young, also a close friend, tells what she felt made Cheryl special to so many. She writes: "I'm not sure why Cheryl chose me to be her friend. Maybe it was because I was new to the school, and she could see that I needed one. Maybe it was because my nickname is 'Sunnie,' and it sounded like we would be a natural fit. I'm not sure of the reason, but what I can say with assurance is that the trajectory of my life was forever altered because she reached out to me.

"In many ways, Cheryl was my first real friend. My family moved around a lot when I was a kid, and Knox, Indiana, was the first place that I stayed long-term.

"Because I had moved so often, I didn't really have an opportunity to build meaningful long-term relationships. The roots were always shallow enough that being uprooted to move to a new community was just another part of life. Cheryl's friendship deepened those roots of community connection so I could withstand the storms of life. Cheryl taught me what it means to be a friend. I felt seen by her. When I came up short, she loved me anyway.

"Cheryl convinced me to join the cross-country team with her by persuading me that it would help condition me for basketball season, and she bribed me with the promise of food! It worked because she saw me and tailored her campaign to align with my personal interests. Cheryl was someone who could be trusted to keep the promises she made, and this minor promise was no different than a more crucial scenario. She held true to her promise on the food and generously shared her plain bagel with me before every cross-country practice!

"Our friendship grew strong because of consistent, positive experiences over a prolonged period of time. She was inclusive and emotionally stable (a rare find in middle school). She noticed if her friends had bad days, she was a great listener who offered useful and thoughtful advice, and she wasn't afraid to call me (or anyone else) out on rude behavior. I didn't ever have to try to 'fit in' if she was around because I knew I actually belonged. There was always a space for me when Cheryl was at the table.

"Our friendship grew during cross-country practices and bus rides. It grew through countless hours of basketball practice. It grew even more when I moved in with her family for a few months during a time when my home life was unstable.

She sat on the bed next to me when I found out I wasn't going to be able to see my dad for Christmas that year, and she hugged me and gave me a safe space to cry. She let me borrow her most precious teddy bear, Dave, to sleep with that night. What Cheryl brought to the table was unmatched. It was as if, somehow, she could see that I was drowning in a situation I didn't have control over, and she reached out her hand and grabbed mine to pull me into the lifeboat, wrapping me in a warm blanket of love. She let me know it was going to be okay . . . that I was going to be okay! I have always attributed this to her being so loved by her family members that she had extra love to pass on to her friends.

"She brought playful energy to our friend group. One time, we got kid's meals from Dairy Queen, and the toy that came with it was a nonfunctional watch that was actually a container for soap and a wand to blow bubbles with. It had a sticker on it for the time, and the hands of this sticker clock said it was 7:51! I know that because for the next six months anyone asked, 'What time is it?" she would enthusiastically reply, 'It's 7:51!'

"If Cheryl had theme music, it would be oldies. She knew all the words to all the songs from that era, and we would sing them together to the radio, which was always tuned to the oldies station in her kitchen. We partnered up for a science project while we were studying ionic and covalent bonds and recorded ourselves singing to the song "Ironic" by Alanis Morissette, except we rewrote the lyrics to say, 'Isn't it ionic' Obviously, it was an artistic masterpiece because the new 'Sunnie and Cher' sang it!

"She loved football and hyped our friend group up to join Powder Puff Football together for a homecoming week tournament. She put the name on the back of her uniform shirt to say 'and Cher,' so when we stood next to each other, our shirts would read 'Sunnie and Cher.'

"Regarding football, Cheryl mentored all of us newbies about how the rules worked for the upcoming flag football tournament. I can distinctly remember the flags on her belt flapping in the wind during practices as she ran the ball in for many touchdowns, partly because she was the only player who understood the rules of the game and partly because of her tenacious nature when she had her heart on winning.

"Cheryl and I liked to sit in the back of biology classes we shared and pass notes to each other. During our first year of high school, I was trying to improve my science grade, so I asked the teacher to move my seat to the front of the class. The first day I sat in the new seat, Cheryl waited until the teacher left the room and moved up to a front-row seat and aggressively raised her hand up in the air waving it back and forth like she had an answer to a question and said, 'I'm Sunnie, I want to *learrrn*!'

"She loved to tease her friends, but it was silly and fun because she was aware enough not to push it past the point of fun for everyone. She prioritized how you felt over the fun of 'getting your goat.' The message Cheryl consistently sent was that you mattered to her, and even if you didn't matter to anyone else in the entire world, being important to Cheryl was somehow enough!"

———— ★ ★ ★ ————

Remembering the good times may initially be a little difficult but, in time, becomes a source of healing, a source of learning more about your child, a source of laughter, and a source to help you find joy in the mourning!

REFLECTIONS: Chapter 19

• What's your favorite memory of the time you spent with your child?

_____

_____

_____

_____

• Name one person who can give you happy memories of your child.

_____

_____

_____

_____

• Ask one person who has happy memories of your child to write those memories down and email them to you.

_____

_____

_____

_____

CHAPTER 20

———— ੭ ഞ ੮ ————

SIGNS FROM ABOVE

As has been pointed out, joy in mourning can be found in many ways, but we must look for it. And sometimes we encounter things that bring us joy at unexpected times and places.

Again, I don't think God does coincidence. I believe everything in our lives is part of His plan. Teaching confirmation class for high schoolers at my church has been such an unbelievable role for me because it has opened my eyes to elements of my faith that I've never thought of before. Of course, biblical scholars have often concluded that there are so many aspects to scripture that we can never totally realize what lessons are in those words, no matter how much we study. Many of those scholars have made studying the scriptures their entire life's work, and they *still* continue to learn. Likewise, even after decades of leading high schoolers to know more about their faith, I continue to learn more about my own faith. I tell my students at the beginning of the year that if we get through this six or seven months later and both they and I are the same, then I haven't done a very good job.

Learning, I've found, leads to change. Not negative change, the kind that would say "I'm leaving the faith based on things I've learned that I didn't know before," but the kind that says, "My faith is stronger now because of what I've learned that I didn't know or didn't understand previously!"

One of the things which absolutely stunned me occurred fifteen years after Cheryl's death as I was teaching class one Sunday. One of the things I often do with the students is to recognize birthdays of the students in the week coming up. In early October 2015, I asked if any of the students had a birthday coming up the next week, and Sara Landa said that hers was coming up on Wednesday. As I thought about it, I realized Wednesday was October 12, and she was going to be fifteen! That meant that she had been born the day Cheryl died!

I was totally bowled over!

With her permission, we talked about that. I learned that she had been born in the morning of that day, so she was probably about twelve hours old when Cheryl died. Another thing I learned was that she had been born in Chicago, and her family didn't move out to Indiana until several years later. What were the chances, I asked my students, that something like this would happen, that she would, all those years later, end up in a class I was teaching a hundred miles from where she was born?

We often talked in the class about all things working together, and this was an incident we discussed for one reason or another throughout the year.

I took this as a message from on high, that I was teaching this class for more than one reason! This part of that reason brought me joy in the mourning!

Over the years, I've encountered more than one story such as this one which has served to both inspire and help me grow in my knowledge and understanding of God's plan for my life.

One of these instances came at an incredibly stressful time in my life when I faced dramatic changes and uncertainty about the future.

By 2022, I had been broadcasting high school sports on the radio for fifty-seven years, first as my vocation, then as my avocation. My new career path was as a financial advisor who owned an extraordinarily successful business that I had built from the ground up, adding two partners along the way.

My partners, Charlie Hasnerl and Devan Wallen, had each joined me at Financial Partners in unique ways. In Charlie's case, I had known his family since I was a kid and knew his grandfather as a successful farmer, businessman, and postmaster from the earliest days of my memory. Ironically, Charlie's father, Ed Hasnerl, gave me my first opportunity in journalism. When I was in high school, as a so-so athlete but a huge fan of high school sports, Ed hired me to write about local sports in his newly established weekly newspaper. That writing gig helped me to no end when I decided to get into radio broadcasting a few years later.

With that knowledge of the Hasnerl family, I got to know Charlie when he graduated from Valparaiso University and moved to Knox, the community where his family roots lay even though he had grown up in Southern Indiana. With my connection at WKVI, the local radio station, I brought him on as a sports analyst, since he had played college football and was also a huge fan of high school sports. That led him to a staff position at the radio station, which he held for a short while before moving on to a sales position at an auto dealership. Shortly after that, he took what was going to be a management position at a manufacturing plant not far away. As a newly married man, Charlie was looking for economic growth in his career and, looking to take care of his family, he became a client of mine at Financial Partners, where we set him up with life insurance and investment opportunities.

Showing up at my office in bibbed overalls after a day's work at the foundry for a review of his portfolio one day, he had several questions which I was able to address. When I asked him if he had any other questions, he pointed to my framed certification as a Chartered Financial Consultant which hung on the wall behind my desk and said, "Yes. How do I get one of those?"

The question surprised me, but I immediately recognized that he was serious and that, with his personality, background in sales, and eagerness to meet and interact with people, he would be an ideal candidate for our business!

In a matter of weeks, I had a new partner at Financial Partners and a new day dawned for both of us.

As our business grew over the next six years, it became obvious that if we were to continue the growth, we needed to add another licensed representative.

We decided that a new representative would have to be someone we knew with local ties, someone who liked meeting and collaborating with people, and someone who had a business background. The person we came to realize who met all those expectations (and more) was Devan Wallen.

Devan Wallen came from a family with ties throughout the community and from a family who had a great number of members who had been in sales, including his grandfather, Leonard Rudd, who had, early in my career, saved my business during the dark days of a recession by providing me with a piece of business that was huge at the time.

In addition to the family ties, Devan had been one of our daughter Cheryl's best friends. Devan gave a very heartfelt eulogy at her funeral.

Devan was finishing his college degree work in marketing when he and his beautiful wife, Elizabeth, were married. They had a destination wedding, then returned home for a very big reception to which Charlie and I were invited. We decided to use the happy occasion as a chance to recruit him for Financial Partners. When he told us at the reception that his future plans were not clear just yet, we asked him to join us for lunch after things settled down. Within a week, Devan decided to join Financial Partners. And the rest, as they say, is history as Financial Partners continued to grow.

———— ★ ★ ★ ————

When you understand that there is no such thing as coincidence, when it comes to our lives, it becomes easier to find the signals that life does go on, and it goes on for a reason. Pursuing those reasons can be fun, exciting, and redemptive as we find joy in the mourning!

REFLECTIONS: Chapter 20

• Name one positive thing which came your way in the immediate aftermath of losing your child.

_____

_____

_____

_____

• Other than the loss of a child, what's the most dramatic thing which happened in your life in the days, months, and years immediately after losing your child?

_____

_____

_____

_____

• Name one way you reacted in a positive manner after losing your child.

_____

_____

_____

_____

CHAPTER 21

MAKING THE RIGHT DECISIONS

Seventeen years after Devan had joined Financial Partners, it became obvious that it was time that I moved on from the endeavors which had occupied my time for decades to moving forward with the Cheryl Lyn Welter Charitable Foundation. My partners and I decided that it would be a suitable time for them to buy my part of the business so that they could continue to grow, and I could move on. My last day at Financial Partners was to be June 30, 2022.

As part of the plan to move on with the foundation, I had realized earlier that my time as a sportscaster at WKVI Radio needed to come to an end as well. I broadcast my last game on June 11, 2022.

When one "retires," I suppose that most people wonder if it's the right thing to do at the right time. As I was stepping away from essentially two careers, both of which I loved, simultaneously, the questions were doubled!

Ending my sportscasting career after fifty-seven years was, obviously, a very public affair. I spoke at length with my listeners at the end of my final game about my feelings and the gratitude that I had for the listeners over the past decades, the athletes who had provided so much excitement, our sponsors who paid the bills while I was having all the fun, and the many families I had gotten to know, covering their kids. Many of those families had taken me in as one of their own, as I was included in many special family days such as graduations, birthdays, and weddings.

Ending my forty-seven-and-a-half years at Financial Partners was a very private affair. I finally got everything moved out of my office at 11:30 p.m. on June 30, 2022, and as I locked the door behind me for the last time, I never felt more alone in my life. No one but me could understand what building that business had meant. The thousands of clients I had helped become financially successful, the families who had become more friends than clients, sharing the ups and downs of our lives together were all the things that I had hoped would be true when I started the business on January 1, 1975. It was fitting, I thought, that I was leaving alone in the dead of night because no one could share that moment with anything close to the emotions I felt. Of course, part of the emotions had to do with whether I had made the *right* decisions, moving on from both of my endeavors simultaneously.

In what turned out to be a brilliant move, we were scheduled to leave for vacation in North Myrtle Beach, South Carolina, bright and early the next morning. Myrtle Beach had been our family vacation spot for thirty-five years, from the time our children were very young until then, when our grandchildren were teenagers! The excitement of going on vacation took precedence in my thoughts on the long drive south.

We had for many years stopped in Asheville, North Carolina, to spend the night before moving on to North Myrtle Beach the next day. After checking in to our hotel, I checked Facebook for the first time all day to see what people were doing and saying. What I found, I took as a signal from Heaven, one that erased any doubt of whether I had made the right decision about moving on to build Cheryl's foundation!

Cami (Parker) Fisher and Cheryl had become friends during their time at Hoosier Girls State between their junior and senior years of high school. Girls State is an exclusive leadership program sponsored by the American Legion and gets outstanding student leaders from all over the state together to learn about our government, our way of life, and what leadership is all about. Cami was from Central Indiana, so she and Cheryl had never met, but they hit it off immediately. They both had been accepted at Purdue University and talked about getting together as soon as they got to campus the next year. Cami had sent flowers for Cheryl's funeral, but we had no contact with her after that.

Kristin (Condon) Ash had been Cheryl's friend since their middle school days when Kristin's family moved back to Knox after her dad took a position as a school administrator in his hometown. Kristin had grown up in Illinois, and though there were family ties in Knox, she really didn't have any friends there. That changed immediately when Cheryl was asked to help Kristin adjust to her new school. They were great friends from that moment on. They both had decided to go to Purdue University after graduation along with several of their friends.

Cami and Kristin met at Purdue and interacted frequently because they were both studying to be teachers. Though Cheryl had been friends with both, they never discovered that connection in their conversations.

When I had announced that I would be wrapping up my two careers to pursue growing the foundation, one of the local TV Stations from South Bend did a feature story on my transition, giving a big boost to Cheryl's foundation.

What I found out when I got to Asheville was that Kristin had posted the TV segment on her Facebook page, and Cari had picked it up. It was only then that Cari and Kristin realized they both had known Cheryl!

I asked myself what the possibility was of those two each knowing Cheryl and each knowing the other for more than twenty years just finding out about the connection as I was wrapping things up and moving in a different direction in my life. I thanked the Lord and Cheryl for giving me a sign that I had, indeed, made the right decision to move on with the foundation and finding a new supporter of Cheryl's efforts to help underprivileged kids!

This only reconfirmed my faith in Romans 8:28: "*All* [emphasis added] things work together for good to those who love God!"

———— ★ ★ ★ ————

Many changes come to our lives which are not directly related to the loss of our child, but dealing with those changes oftentimes does circle back to that loss. It forces us to look at all aspects of our lives and how they fit into God's plan, including that loss. If we embrace change as a way to grow, then we are truly on the path to finding joy in the mourning.

REFLECTIONS: Chapter 21

• Name one "coincidence" that occurred after you lost your child that affected you in ways you didn't expect.

_____

_____

_____

_____

• Name one person you believe felt your loss in a unique way.

_____

_____

_____

_____

• Name one change which came into your life other than the colossal impact of losing your child.

_____

_____

_____

_____

CHAPTER 22

———— ༈ ————

WHAT HAVE YOU DONE
FOR ME LATELY?

One of the five stages of grief is the bargaining stage, where we essentially say, "God, if you let my child live, <u>I'll always going forward!" or "God, if you let my child live, I'll never again!"</u>

This bargaining phase may be the most difficult of the stages of grief because we have to believe something so far-fetched (like reversing the most drastic thing imaginable, something that has already happened); which, in our heart of hearts, is something we know that cannot come true.

When something tragic happens, be it the loss of a child or anyone else close to us, the loss of a job or career we've sustained for a long time, or the tornado that destroyed our home and all our belongings, the question is always, "Where do we go from here?"

In my case, it took me several years to address that question. When I did get it answered, our financial services business really began to grow and thrive, and the Cheryl Lyn Welter Charitable Foundation did as well!

Unfortunately, too many people in grief, no matter the reason for their grief, get stuck on square one and never ask that question. Yet, if we are to get through our grief and go toward growth, we must constantly ask the question, "Where do we go from here?"

But that's a question which should be asked even when things are going well.

In business, there's a probing question which follows every loss or every gain when the business leader says, "What have you done for me lately?"

If a business has a major setback, the question is: "What have you done for me lately?"

If a business has the biggest sale in its history the question is: "That's nice, but what have you done for me lately?"

In other words, the business leader or business owner is saying, "Life goes on, so what's your plan to make sure it gets better and not worse?"

Every business salesperson knows they're only as good as their last sale, and no matter how big that sale was, they need to know where the next sale is coming from. In the case of a sale *loss*, the sales manager has to say, "That was a great sale you almost closed, but what have you done for me lately?"

The same is true in the grieving process. At some point, whoever has felt the loss has to ask of themselves, "Okay, so what have you done for me lately?" In other words, what are the next steps we're going to take so as not to be backed into a corner where all the negatives of what just happened will continue to inflame our very existence.

So, when the time comes, and the grief is overwhelming, you need to ask yourself the equivalent question of "What have you done for me lately?" The question for this situation is "Okay, so what's next? Am I going to withdraw from life and replay all the pain and negativity of my loss, or am I going to choose the sixth stage of grief, *growth*?"

———— ★ ★ ★ ————

Perhaps the biggest lesson after the loss of a child (or any significant loss we experience) is that life *does* go on, so the challenge becomes how are we going to deal with life going forward as we seek to find joy in the mourning!

REFLECTIONS: Chapter 22

• Name one answer to the question "Where do we go from here?" that you will go to work on in the next twenty-four hours.

_____

_____

_____

_____

• Name one person who can help you to execute your answer to the above question.

_____

_____

_____

_____

• How will answering that question help you to grow?

_____

_____

_____

_____

CHAPTER 23

WHAT NOT TO DO

One of the most difficult parts of dealing with the death of a child is working on what has to be done in the aftermath of the loss, and the flip side of that is what you *shouldn't* do.

On the list of what *not* to do after a loss like this is to forget your lost child's siblings!

The most devastating result of the grieving process for me was that I didn't seek to help Cheryl's siblings with their grieving process. Her oldest sister, Susan, was working in Washington, DC. She was on her own there and had to return to an apartment and a lifestyle which didn't offer a lot of support for her. Fortunately, the congressman for whom she worked allowed her to take all the time she needed before returning to work, which, in the end, constituted about three and a half weeks. Even though I drove her back to DC and her professional life, I didn't leave her with any kind of plan which could help her cope with the loss of her sister. In retrospect, I should have set goals for when we would get together on a regular basis.

Cheryl's sister, Laura, was in her senior year of college when the accident occurred. Since she lived on campus, she rarely came home during the week. For some reason, however, she came home on that Thursday and was with Cheryl for a brief period before the accident. There again, however, once Laura returned to college after the funeral, we didn't have a plan to regularly get together and help each other through the grieving process.

Cheryl's brother, Nathan, was fifteen months younger than Cheryl, and the two were best friends. He was just sixteen years old at the time he lost his sister, and not being one to wear his heart on his sleeve, he kept things inside. Unfortunately, because he and I were not as close as I would have liked, I was of no help to him in the grieving process. I should have known that, as devastating as the loss was to me, an adult, the loss, the questions, and the inability to understand was multiplied for a teenager who had just lost his best friend. Sadly, the challenges for Nathan grew as the years went by, and I still was no help.

In my subsequent efforts in counseling parents who have lost children, one of the first things I tell them is to be aware of the needs of siblings, no matter their age or their circumstances.

There's an old song, written by Bill Anderson, called "A Lot of Things Different" which reminisces about the past. The song haunts me because I realize that I would change a lot of things about how I dealt with my own grief, to be sure, but especially with the grief of Cheryl's siblings.

As you begin the journey of moving on without your lost loved one, there are many choices to be made. Some are easier than others, but all can affect our lives in dramatic ways.

The best choice you can make is to wait at least six months after your loss before making any long-range decisions which can change your life dramatically. This includes financial decisions, personal decisions, and emotional decisions.

In my work as a financial consultant, my partners and I made this a standard part of our advice to our clients who lost a close loved one, particularly a spouse: "Don't make any substantial investment decision in the first six months," we'd say, "And don't make any emotional decisions, either."

Too often, we saw people who lost a spouse begin to spend money recklessly, buying things which their deceased partner had dreamed about. Likewise, we saw a number of newly widowed individuals quickly remarry after losing a spouse. Rarely do those kinds of relationships last.

Yes, there often are steps which need to be taken for purposes the couple may have discussed before the first spouse died. For instance, if the house needs a new roof, which is going to be an expensive affair, obviously you would need to go forth with those plans before the house develops major problems. But that new luxury van you had planned to have to travel all over the country like you'd always dreamed of? That may not be a good buy, since you, the surviving spouse, are probably not going to use the van for a cross-county adventure anytime soon.

Now, if you were buying the new van to replace an old worn-out vehicle as well as to have a great traveling vehicle, that need may still exist. But you may want to buy a smaller, more efficient vehicle rather than a larger one.

How people grieve is as individual as the number of losses. One of the things I perceived very shortly after the loss of our daughter was that no one seemed to understand what I was going through . . . what I was feeling! Eventually, I came to the understanding that each person who has the experience of losing a child manages it differently and that this was probably true for anyone going through grief of any kind. This stems, I came to believe, from the fact that we are all individuals with our own thoughts, our own history, and our own feelings. And it's also probably true that everyone manages virtually *everything* differently than anyone else because of our uniqueness as human beings.

———— ★ ★ ★ ————

Understanding that life goes on after the loss of a child is a lesson which takes time, effort, and energy. It also requires us to be brutally honest with ourselves about what we have done and are doing to deal with the realities of life. No matter how long it's been since our loss, understanding what we should *not* be doing is as important as understanding what we *should* be doing if we're going to find joy in the mourning!

REFLECTIONS: Chapter 23

• What is one big decision you have made (or need to make) after losing your child, and what long-term effect could that decision have?

_____

_____

_____

_____

• What characteristics does each sibling have that are most _like_ your lost child?

_____

_____

_____

_____

• What characteristics does each sibling have that are different?

_____

_____

_____

_____

CHAPTER 24

FIND A NEED AND FILL IT

The day when parents lose a child never ends. The pain never goes away. The mourning never stops.

In closing, I realize that finding joy in the mourning is not easy, but it *is* simple. The simplicity lies in living the lives we once dreamed of, finding things and, more importantly, people to enjoy! We also need to find purpose again, and that can be done simply by looking at the needs of others that we can help fill.

In the end, finding joy in the mourning is not about *us*! It's about learning about life and how we manage the good times and the bad. It's about how we can help others. It's about learning God's plan for our lives.

Having spent most of my life in sales, I remember the old salesman's trick to finding success: Find a need and fill it! To find success in finding joy in the mourning is as simple as that too: Find a place that needs joy and provide it! That includes in your life, the lives of people with whom you can share your joy, and the joy of having your child with you as long as you did . . . whether that's a short number of years, a lot of years, or only days or hours!

The key to seeking and finding joy in the mourning is to ask yourself this question:

If God had come to you before your lost child was born and said, "I'm giving you this child, to have and to hold, to love and to teach, but, after so many years, I'm taking the child back to be with me." If He also told you about all the pain, suffering, and doubts you have suffered since the loss of your child—the anguish, the second-guessing of yourself, and the sleepless nights you've experienced since losing your child—would you choose to never have had the child and, therefore, been able to avoid all of the things which went wrong and caused you untold pain? Or would you have taken the child and accepted all that came with losing that child? In other words, if God had told you all those things and then said to you, "Deal or no deal." Would you take the deal?

Only you can answer that question. Was having your child for the limited time you experienced worth it? Would you do it all over again?

I have found that finding purpose, joy, and focus in your life after losing a child can be facilitated by scripture. I've never read the Bible cover to cover, but I have found several quotes from scripture which have helped me in multiple situations, as they had come to me in multiple ways.

Consider 2 Timothy 4:7: "I have kept the faith."

This was the scripture used at the funeral of my father, who passed away at the age of ninety after a very difficult life in which he had been institutionalized for the last twenty-five years. Referring to his difficult life, Pastor William Vogt said about him, "Through it all . . . he kept the faith."

I adopted that quote early in my sportscasting career, when, at the end of each game, I told my listeners,

"Whether you win or whether you lose, always . . . keep the faith, fans!"

Romans 8:28 tells us that "All things work together for good to those who love God."

As you know, this was on a plaque given to us as a wedding gift and has hung on our wall ever since. It became the driving force behind creating and maintaining the Cheryl Lyn Welter Family Charitable Foundation.

Then, there's Psalm 30:5: "Joy comes in the morning."

This became important to me after hearing it at the funeral of a friend when it dawned on me that if you just spelled it "mourning" instead of "morning," it could expand the meaning of that scripture to be an encouragement to many. Of course, that's where the title of this book came from. My hope is that it can go forward to give hope to those who have lost a child.

———— ⋆ ★ ⋆ ————

Finding joy in the mourning is tied to finding meaning in your life after losing a child. Finding a need for all the things you have to offer and then filling that need can benefit both you and those whose lives you will touch in a positive way.

To the many people who shared their experiences with me after losing a child, I can say that, whether you realized it or not, you have already found a need and filled it. I had the need to share my story and to learn the stories of others, and you filled that need by listening to my story and sharing yours with me. And to the many who encouraged the writing of this book, you, too, found that need in me and filled it with your encouragement, your support, and your love. Your stories, your love, and your encouragement will stay with me forever.

To all in need of what this book conveys, I encourage you to "Keep the Faith" and to continue to seek joy in the mourning!

REFLECTIONS: Chapter 24

• What is one need that you see that you can fill for someone else?

_____

_____

_____

_____

• What three Bible verses give you solace and encouragement?

_____

_____

_____

_____

• Who will be the first person with whom you will share the lessons you've learned while reading this book?

_____

_____

_____

_____

ACKNOWLEDGMENTS

Though I've been in the business of communication all my life, starting by selling peaches off the back of a pickup truck in the hills of Alabama when I was twelve years old and continuing as a radio broadcaster and financial advisor in later life, I never thought of writing a book.

As a radio sportscaster, I learned to talk in sound bites, describing what was happening on the playing field in fifteen seconds or less. In my role as a financial advisor, I could use an "elevator speech" to describe how I could help potential clients by describing what I did in thirty seconds, the duration of a typical elevator ride. Writing forty thousand words for a book was not something I would have ever thought possible.

Over the fifty-seven years I spent broadcasting high school sports, I often was told I should write a book about my many experiences and the great athletes and games I covered. I always begged off because my memory wasn't good enough to remember back that far.

When I did begin to consider writing a book, however, it was only loosely tied to my sportscasting and financial advisor careers. It was God who put the idea in my head that I could perhaps help other people who had lost children because of how we started a charitable foundation in our daughter Cheryl's memory to find joy in the mourning.

This book, I've come to realize, came about not because someone said I should write a book about dealing with grief but because of the people in my life who have helped me in many ways become who I am.

The first person who set me on my life's path that led to this book was my mom. Lou Ellen Atchison Welter never got past the third grade in school, never learned to drive a car, and was crippled by polio at an early age, but she raised seven children as a single mom in a broken-down, old farmhouse that didn't have electricity, running water, or indoor plumbing. But each one of those children became productive members of society. She taught us to work hard, be honest, and believe in our own abilities and that those characteristics would make life worth living. And, oh yes, she taught me how to keep the memory of a lost child alive.

Two years before I was born, she lost a two-day-old child, but she made sure that we always remembered our sister, Jeanette. Learning from Mom's teaching, I became determined that people would remember our lost daughter, Cheryl.

I believe we all have a handful of people in our lives who help shape who we become by the way they help us become better people.

That handful of people for me included "Puma" Bob Hayes, who taught me how to do sports play-by-play on the radio. He always emphasized that a lack of knowledge could be made up for by enthusiasm, so while I didn't have the greatest knowledge of the games, I could be identified by my enthusiasm for the action. Another broadcast partner, Dave Bard, helped me develop a professionalism in sportscasting that I hope I was able to articulate over the years.

My life was forever changed by Congressman Earl Landgrebe, who hired me as his press secretary, taking me to Washington, DC, to work on Capitol Hill, something that a poor kid from poverty-stricken rural Indiana could never have imagined. Walking with and talking with four presidents of the United States helped me believe that anything was possible.

Bob Goble, whom I met as I was broadcasting high school sports while he was officiating games, took me in a totally different direction after my experience in Washington when he got me started as a financial advisor. He encouraged me to start my own company, where I enjoyed a satisfying career for more than forty-seven years.

My wife, Becky, who has put up with me for more than a half-century of sometimes challenging married life, has been the unsung hero in my life. While I was on the road, broadcasting more than three thousand ball games and servicing my financial clients at meetings across the country, she was home raising our kids virtually alone.

I owe a debt of gratitude to those who allowed me to tell their stories of finding joy in the mourning in this book after they lost children. To Al Breyfogle, Tim and Melinda Roth, Deb Carmean Johnson, Bernadette Welter Manuel, Julie West, Jo Whitesell Fisher, Teresa Mago, Shirley Young-Walters, and others, thank you for teaching me more about finding joy in the mourning than I ever could have taught you.

I also want to acknowledge Becky Bailey, who became one of the biggest supporters of the Cheryl Lyn Welter Charitable Foundation based on her own life experiences that led her to work for underprivileged children and their mothers. She taught me how to be optimistic in setting financial goals for the foundation and to stretch my thinking.

And then there's the support I received from literally thousands of others. These were the listeners of my sportscasts over those fifty-seven years: the coaches and athletes whom I got to know and the players and their families, so many of whom included me as part of their families over the years. I'm also grateful to my clients from all over the country who trusted me as their financial advisor for decades and who became more like friends than clients as we shared the ups and downs of our lives. Know that all of you played a role in this book as you helped me become who I am.

I'd also like to thank the one person who not only encouraged me to write this book but also helped coach me through it. Stephanie L. Jones was a professional organizer when we first met. I didn't even know there *was* such a thing as a professional organizer, but she came to my office one day to show me how to clean the pile on my desk and get organized. Though I still struggle with keeping my desk clean, Stephanie became a coach whom I confer with weekly as we set goals and devise plans to meet those goals. Stephanie has overcome her own challenges in life to become one of the most positive people I've ever met. This book would not have been written without her support, encouragement, and advice. Whatever success it may have, much of the credit goes to Stephanie.

Of course, the majority of the credit for this book and any success I may have in life goes to God. He has appeared to me many times but usually disguises himself as everyday people who have had an uncommon effect on my life. It's because He lives that I can face tomorrow, and because He lives, all fear is gone! He has truly given me the ability to find joy in the mourning!

APPENDIX

Helping others is something which has played a big part in the grieving process for me, and that includes helping others through the Cheryl Lyn Welter Charitable Foundation.

Here are some of the stories from those who have received grants from the foundation which signal that Cheryl's life goal of helping others is being actualized:

Two Knox Elementary school teachers received grants to provide playground additions to benefit students in wheelchairs and walkers and other special needs children.

A third-grade teacher at North Judson-San Pierre Elementary School was awarded a grant to be used for a "Survive the Summer" pack for especially needy students!

A paraprofessional at Knox High School was awarded a grant for Knox students to attend an autism camp that provides them two weeks of fun and learning activities with children from eight other school districts.

A special education teacher at West Central High School received a grant to replace a worn-out walker for one of her students! This new equipment will allow him to be more independent.

At Knox Elementary School, three teachers were awarded grants. One was used to provide educational kits which carried some underprivileged elementary students through the "learning at home" period brought on by COVID-19 and beyond. Another was used to provide blankets, sheets, pillows, bedtime books, and stuffed animals for three elementary children who lost all their belongings in a house fire. The third grant was used to provide food baskets for six underprivileged middle school students who were not at school—but getting school meals—during the virus.

Two Culver Community Elementary teachers used funds from a grant to fill supply bags that helped 115 children from low-income families to continue to learn and have fun during the pandemic.

A Knox High School teacher used a grant with her Principles of Human Services students to create comfort-item backpacks for children in the community who were taken away from their parents by authorities seeking to protect the children. The goal is that at the time of separation, the child would be given a bag that includes items that will make the hard time easier to manage. This is a project that her students felt passionate about because of firsthand experiences for some, and it gave every student an opportunity to get involved in helping others. The students put together these great sacks which they called "Cheryl's Care Kits." They were able to make twenty-four kits! Each kit included a backpack, blanket, coloring book, colored pencils, a teddy bear, Gatorade, cheddar popcorn, a chewy bar, fruit snacks, a flashlight, a mini heart stress ball, and a toothbrush and toothpaste.

A Kankakee Valley Middle School teacher used a grant to purchase a pair of EnChroma glasses for colorblind students at the middle school to use during Art and FACS classes. EnChroma glasses help these students be able to see some colors better, which will help students with their projects. Students expressed difficulty and frustration in picking colors for projects when they aren't quite sure what the colors are. This helped colorblind students take more pride in their projects. The cost of these glasses makes them far out of reach for many families.

Multiple Care Closets have been created and supported at many rural schools with grants from the Cheryl Lyn Welter Family Charitable Foundation. These Care Closets hold hygiene items, clothes, food, medicine, and many other basic necessities which some students are not able to get at home.

One of the first grants awarded by the foundation went to a teacher who had two underprivileged students who wanted to get into the Certified Nursing Assistant (CNA) program which required fees and other costs in order to be admitted. When the teacher applied for the grant so that these students could take that step, she said that it changed their lives. Neither student, the teacher explained, had any aspirations to have a better life until this opportunity was opened to them. Knowing that the CNA designation could be the first step toward earning a registered nurse degree, the students were overwhelmed with the opportunity presented to them by these grants.

One teacher who received a grant from the foundation used the funds to purchase alternate student seating. She explained the value of this by saying, "Many students have focusing issues from being understimulated at home in low-income families. Alternate seating allows them to move to get to the optimum learning level through motion. These seats include wobbly stools, exercise yoga balls with a base, chair cushions, and scoop chairs. By offering these chairs as a seating option, student learning can be more successful. For some, it is motivation to come to school because it is their turn to use the chair!

NOTES

1. James R. Welter, "Mourning Has Broken. Living Through Grief" (1994).

2. Sigmund Freud, (1926d [1925]), "Inhibitions, Symptoms, and Anxiety," in Sigmund Freud, James Strachey, Anna Freud, and Carrie Lee Rothgeb, *The Standard Edition of the Complete Psychological Works of Sigmund Freud, Vol. 20* (London: Hogarth Press and the Institute of Psycho-Analysis, 1953), 75–172.

3. Doug Manning, *Don't Take My Grief Away from Me* (Edmond, OK: In Sight Books, 1983), 53.

4. Manning, *Don't Take My Grief,* 53.

5. Erich Lindemann, "Symptomatology and the Management of Acute Grief" *American Journal of Psychiatry,* 101 (1944): 141–148.

6. Marissa Conrad, "Anticipatory Grief: What It Is and How to Cope," updated September 29, 2023, *Forbes* Health, https://www.forbes.com/health/mind/what-is-anticipatory-grief/.

7. Manning, *Don't Take My Grief,* 53.

8. Harriet Sarnoff Schiff, *The Bereaved Parent* (New York: Crown Publishers, 1977), 57.

9. The Compassionate Friends 2006 survey results (see compassionatefriends.org) in Sandy Fox, *Creating a*

New Normal After the Death of a Child (Bloomington, IN: iUniverse, 2010), 144.

10. Schiff, *Bereaved Parent*, in Fox, *Death of a Child,* 144.

11. "Grief." Noah Webster and Noah Porter, *An American Dictionary of the English Language,* eds. Chauncy A. Goodrich and C Merriam (Springfield, MA: George and Charles Merriam,1860). PDF, https://www.loc.gov/tiem/40023586/.

12. Elisabeth Kübler-Ross, *On Death and Dying* (New York: Macmillan Publishing, 1969), 51, 63, 93, 97, 123.

13. Candi K. Cann, "Grief Theories and the Thinking Behind Them," Roundglass Living, https://roundglassliving.com/grieving/articles/grief-theories-and-the-thinking-behind-them#:~:text=Influenced%20by%20K%C3%BCbler%2DRoss%2C%20but,emphasis%20of%20Calvinist%20work%20ethics.

14. Kübler-Ross, *Death and Dying*, 124.

15. "Growth." *Merriam-Webster.com,* November 29, 2023, https://www.merriam-webster.com/dictionary/growth.

16. Alexander Johnson, "Five Principles of Growth," *Science Oxygen* (blog), September 9, 2022, https://scienceoxygen.com/.

17. Manning, *Don't Take My Grief*, 53.

REACH OUT TO THE AUTHOR

You may order additional copies of

JOY IN THE MOURNING

Visit our website at www.cherylskidsfund.org
or call 574-850-8853.

If you are looking for a speaker for your church, club,
or business,
Harold Welter has extensive public speaking
experience, challenging and inspiring his audiences with
stories gleaned from his fifty-seven years as a
sportscaster, his role as a financial advisor and his
experience working on Capitol Hill in Washington, DC,
as well as his role as executive director of a unique
nonprofit organization.

Contact Harold via e-mail at hawelter@yahoo.com or
by text to 574-850-8853.

www.ingramcontent.com/pod-product-compliance
Lightning Source LLC
Chambersburg PA
CBHW070121100426
42744CB00010B/1888